Alexis Caswell
From the Author
Jan. 16. 1871

PSALMS.

THE

PSALMS.

THE COMMON VERSION REVISED

FOR

THE AMERICAN BIBLE UNION,

WITH

AN INTRODUCTION AND OCCASIONAL NOTES.

BY THOMAS J. CONANT.

New York:
AMERICAN BIBLE UNION, No 32 GREAT JONES STREET.
LONDON: TRÜBNER & CO., 60 PATERNOSTER ROW.

1871.

TO THE READER.

The reader, who may take the trouble to compare the following version with the Hebrew text, will please bear in mind, that it is a revision of the common English version, and not an independent translation. No other changes have been made than seemed necessary to the clear expression of the sense. It has been the writer's aim, in all cases, to give the true sense of the Hebrew text, but with as little change as possible of the familiar phraseology of the common version. Mere verbal correspondence with the original has not been sought, either in words or in their order, except where emphasis or point of expression seems to require it.

The Hebrew text followed in the revision is that of Baer's new critical edition of the Hebrew Psalter.*

The notes are not intended to be exegetical, but only to furnish such occasional hints as seem necessary to the intelligent reading of the psalm.

Where there is an alternative rendering or textual reading, in the margin, it is given as of nearly equal authority with that in the text, and may be substituted for it. The text and margin are equally parts of the revision.

Where a word used in the first member is, by the Hebrew construction, necessarily implied in the second, it is inserted without brackets, the sentence being incomplete without it.

The Introduction is not designed to be a critical discussion of the topics treated of, but only to give such information as may be useful to the general reader.

---

* Liber Psalmorum Hebraicus. Textum masorethicum accuratius quam adhuc factum est expressit, brevem de accentibus metricis institutionem præmisit, notas criticas adjecit S. Baer. Præfatus est Fr. Delitzsch. 1861.

The following are the later critical and exegetical works on the Psalms, used in the preparation of this revised version, as representing the present state of critical learning.

Maurer, Psalmi (Commentarius Criticus, vol. iii.). 1838.

Vaihinger, die Psalmen metrisch übersetzt und erklärt. 1845.

Delitzsch, Symbolæ ad psalmos illustrandos isagogicæ. 1846.

Phillips, the Psalms in Heb., with Crit., Exeget., and Philolog. Com. 1846.

Lengerke, die fünf Bücher der Psalmen. 1847.

Hengstenberg, Commentar über die Psalmen, 1ster Band, 2te Aufl. 1849.

Alexander, the Psalms Translated and Explained. 1850.

Olshausen, die Psalmen erklärt. 1853.

De Wette, Commentar über die Psalmen, 5te Aufl. von Bauer. 1856.

Hitzig, die Psalmen übersetzt und ausgelegt. 1863.

Kamphausen (Bunsen's Bibelwerk). 1863.

Ewald, die Psalmen erklärt, 3te Ausg. 1866.

Hupfeld, die Psalmen übersetzt und ausgelegt, 2te Aufl. von Riehm. 1867.

Delitzsch, die Psalmen, neue Ausarbeitung (Bibl. Com. 4ter Theil). 1867.

Ehrt, Abfassungszeit und Abschluss des Psalters. 1869.

Moll, die Psalter, 1ste Hälfte (Lange's Bibelwerk). 1869.

Perowne's recent work on the Psalms has been accessible to me only in the second volume. Dr. Noyes' elegant version of the Psalms differs too much from mine, in the theory of translation, to be of use to me.

T. J. CONANT.

OCTOBER, 1870.

INTRODUCTION.

§ 1.

Divine Authority and Inspiration of the Book.

In respect to its divine authority and inspiration, the Book of Psalms rests on the same grounds as the other canonical books of the Old Testament, namely, the attestation of Christ and his inspired apostles. It belonged to that collection of sacred writings,* denominated in the New Testament, "the Word of God" (Mark 7 : 13), "the Oracles of God" (Rom. 3 : 2), "the Scriptures" (John 5 : 39; Acts 17 : 2), and "the Holy Scriptures" (Rom. 1 : 2; 2 Tim. 3 : 15). Of these, collectively, the Apostle Paul says (2 Tim. 3 : 16), "All Scripture is given by inspiration of God" (is inspired by God); and they are referred to by Christ himself, and by his accredited apostles, as the authoritative teachings of the Divine Spirit. See, for example, such passages as Matt. 5 : 17–19; John 5 : 39; Rom. 3 : 2; Matt. 22 : 43, and Mark 12 : 36; 2 Tim. 3 : 16; 1 Pet. 1 : 10–12; 2 Pet. 1 : 21.

Of no portion of the Old Testament is this attestation more direct and explicit, than of the Book of Psalms. In Matt. 21 : 42, the Savior expressly recognizes it as part of that divine Canon: "Did ye never read in the Scriptures, The stone which the builders rejected, the same is become the head of the corner?" In this quotation (from Ps. 118 ; 22, 23) the book is included in "the Scriptures," as an integral part of them. Referring to it in Mark 12 : 36 by its customary designation (compare Heb. 4 : 7), and quoting its language, he expressly asserts that David said it "by the Holy Ghost," or, (as it may be rendered) "in the Holy Spirit," meaning, by

* The proof that the Hebrew Scriptures, as they have come down to us, constituted this collection, and that the Book of Psalms was an integral part of it, belongs to a general Introduction to the writings of the Old Testament.

direction, or under the influence and guidance, of the Holy Spirit. Of the book as a whole he again says, in Luke 24 : 44, "All things must be fulfilled, which were written in the Law of Moses, and in the Prophets, and in the Psalms, concerning me;" placing it in the same rank with the most authoritative portions of the Old Testament, and recognizing its divine teachings respecting himself.

A similar attestation is given by the sacred writers of the New Testament; as in Acts 4 : 25, "Who by the mouth of thy servant David hast said," referring to the book by its familiar and customary designation; and in Heb. 3 : 7, "As the Holy Spirit says, To-day if ye will hear his voice" (Ps. 95 : 7).

Thus the Savior and his apostles affirm of the book, what the Royal Psalmist, the principal writer, says of himself: "The Spirit of the Lord spoke by me, and his word was in my tongue" (2 Sam. 23 : 2).

§ 2.

Collection of the Psalms.

The Book of Psalms is a collection, or rather a series of collections, of the sacred poetry of the nation, designed for private devotion and for the public worship of the sanctuary. The whole consists of five distinct collections, made at different times, in the order in which they now stand. The close of each is indicated by a doxology.*

1. The collection first made included Pss. 2–41,† almost all of which are noted as David's, and was doubtless intended to be a collection of his psalms. There are but three which are not noted as his, namely the 2d, 10th, and 33d; and nothing in their contents forbids the supposition that he was the writer.

2. The second (Pss. 42–72) is a collection of levitical psalms (42–50), seven by the sons of Korah and one by Asaph, chiefly of a national character, followed by nineteen psalms of David, and three of which the writer is not named, closing with one by Solomon. The appended note, "The prayers of David the son of Jesse are ended," was probably inserted here when the next collection was added, in order to show where the productions of the Royal Psalmist, as then collected, closed.

* The several collections are also distinguished, in part, by characteristic peculiarities in the use of the divine names. (See *Smith's Bible Dictionary*, art. Psalms, fourth paragraph.)

† The first psalm appears to have been intended as an introduction to the whole when collected into one book, most probably in the time of Ezra.

3. The third (Pss. 73–89) contains a collection of eleven psalms by Asaph, and one of four psalms by the sons of Korah, and one psalm by Ethan. Only the 86th Psalm is ascribed to David; and with this exception, the whole collection is from those connected with the temple service, and was probably added as a supplement to the two former ones, which were chiefly from the pen of the Royal Psalmist.

4. The fourth (Pss. 90–106) includes but three whose writers are mentioned, namely, the 90th Psalm by Moses, and the 101st and 103d Psalms by David. Except these three, they are very general in their contents, and were apparently intended for use in the temple service and at national festivals.

5. The fifth (Pss. 107–150) was a collection, apparently, of all the psalms extant when it was made, and not included in the previous ones. It contains fifteen psalms of David* and one of Solomon, and twenty-eight of which the writers are not given. It includes smaller separate collections of an earlier date; the Pilgrim Songs, fifteen in number (Pss. 120–134), and Pss. 111–118 designed for the temple service and for festival occasions. There is also a collection of David's psalms placed by themselves (Pss. 138–145), and the whole is appropriately closed with songs of praise to Jehovah (Pss. 146–150).

The evident grouping of psalms related in contents, design, or authorship, shows that the arrangement in the several collections was systematically made. It is also seen that minor collections had previously been made from time to time, and were incorporated in those which now compose the book.

The object of each collection is apparent from the above view. It also accounts for the repetition of the same psalm in different parts of the book, as in the case of Pss. 14 and 53. Some have regarded Pss. 57 and 108 as a similar case. But only the last five verses of the former and the first five of the latter are the same in both, with some verbal variations; and as both are by the same writer, it is more probable that he employed in part the same language in composing two different psalms.

At what time or by whom these several collections were made, is unknown. In the time of Hezekiah, the psalms authorized to be sung in the temple service were those of David and of Asaph the Seer (2 Chron. 29 : 30).

* It has been suggested, that by the name David, in the titles to psalms of the third, fourth, and fifth collections, may be meant his representative in the royal head of his family, representing his name and sovereignty at the time when the psalm was written. Compare this use of the name in 1 Kings 12 : 16; Hos. 3 : 5; Jer. 30 : 9; Ezek. 34 : 23, 24. (See *Smith's Bible Dictionary*, art. Psalms, last half of the seventh paragraph.)

From this it may naturally be inferred, that the psalms of the first three collections were not then disposed in their present arrangement. The last two collections could not have been made till after the captivity, as is shown by the style and subject of some of the psalms included in them. The whole book could not, therefore, have received its present form long before the completion of the Old Testament Canon, or about the time of Ezra. In the Greek version by the Seventy, completed more than two centuries before Christ, these five collections are indicated as in the present Hebrew text.

The body of sacred poetry, authorized by the Royal Psalmist and Asaph the Seer to be used in the worship of the sanctuary, was increased from time to time, as divinely authorized, under the direction of a succession of Prophets and High-Priests, through whose agency the temple service was maintained. The collections thus formed were included in the sacred Canon, most probably by the authority of Ezra. Our inability to determine in every case the writer of a psalm, or by whom the several collections were made or the arrangement of the whole was completed, does not affect the authority of this collection of sacred poetry as a part of divine revelation. This is attested by the declarations of Christ and his inspired apostles, as already stated in the first section.

§ 3.

Titles of the Psalms.

Nearly all of the psalms, with only thirty three exceptions, (Pss. 42 and 43 being reckoned as one,) have titles or inscriptions prefixed to them. The object of the title is chiefly to designate the writer of the psalm. But some designate the one to whom it was committed for use in the temple service; others the character or style of the composition, as a psalm, a song, a prayer, as didactic, or plaintive, etc.; others the occasion on which it was composed, and its subject; others the tune or melody to which it was sung, or the accompanying instrument; and in some, several of these objects are combined. They are of great value to the interpreter, particularly in determining the writer and age, and sometimes the occasion and subject of a psalm. The correctness of their statements is now admitted by the best interpreters.

§ 4.

Writers of the Psalms.

The writers of one hundred of the psalms are named in the titles prefixed to them. Of these seventy-three are ascribed to David. As a greater number were written by him than by all the others named in the book, and as he was the most distinguished of them all, the whole collection sometimes bears his name, as in Heb. 4 : 7.

Twelve of the psalms (namely, Ps. 50, and Pss. 73–83) are ascribed to Asaph. The most distinguished of this name, cotemporary with David, is called in 2 Chron. 29 : 30 "Asaph the Seer," one whom God commissioned to declare his will (1 Sam. 9 : 9), and is there named in connection with David as a writer of psalms to be used in the temple worship. Psalms of a later period, bearing this name, may have been written by another of the family of Asaph (2 Chron. 35 : 15), which continued to be mentioned with distinction till after the return from the captivity (Neh. 7 : 44).

Eleven of the psalms (namely, Pss. 42 and 43 reckoned as one, Pss. 44–49, Pss. 84, 85, 87, 88) bear the name of a levitical family of singers, the sons of Korah. They were a distinguished family at the period of David's reign, and noted for their attachment to him and to his throne. They were among those who identified themselves with his cause and fortunes at Ziklag, when he was pressed by the whole power of Saul (1 Chron. 12 : 1, 6). The psalms ascribed to them breathe the same zeal for his person, and for the divinely constituted sovereignty represented in him.

The similarity of some of these psalms to those of David, in the general tone of sentiment and the historical circumstances referred to, have led some to regard him as the writer, and the title as indicating the delivery of the psalm, "to (or, for) the sons of Korah." But he is in none of them named as the writer, as elsewhere in connection with the delivery of the psalm; and the language is the natural utterance of one who shared his fortunes and his sentiments, and gave expression to both.

Heman the Ezrahite is named as the writer of Ps. 88, and Ethan the Ezrahite, of Ps. 89. Solomon's name is prefixed to Pss. 72 and 127. Moses is named as the writer of the 90th Psalm.

The psalms belonging to the later periods of the kingdom are most of them without the name of the writer. Their date is ascertained, in some by the subject, in others approximately by the general manner and style of expression. For, as a general rule, the earlier psalms exhibit more freedom and originality of expression, and more abruptness and condensation of thought, and hence are more difficult. The later psalms, as might be expected, are composed more in the language acquired by imitation and culture, and hence are more plain and perspicuous in style.

§ 5.

Historical Divisions of the Psalms.

The psalms should be studied with reference to the four historical periods to which (with the exception of the 90th Psalm by Moses) they respectively belong. They fall naturally into the following four divisions: 1. Those of the period preceding David's elevation to the throne, from the time when he was anointed for the sovereignty of Israel, "and the Spirit of the Lord came upon him" (1 Sam. 16 : 13). 2. Those written during his personal reign. 3. Those of the subsequent period extending to the captivity. 4. Those written during the captivity and after the return.

A minute acquaintance with the history of these several periods is necessary in determining the age to which a psalm belongs, when there is no title indicating it, and in interpreting its historical and personal allusions. This is especially applicable to the psalms of David, where many of the sentiments and allusions can not be rightly and fully understood, without an intimate acquaintance with the domestic circumstances of the kingdom.

The commencement of his reign found the kingdom in a very depressed condition; subjected, in great part, to the surrounding heathen nations, and without any principle of union to secure concert of action against their further encroachments. The nation was divided between the adherents of the house of Saul and those of David, and was sunk in the rudeness and barbarism consequent on a long period of external and internal wars. One of the first acts of David's reign, when at length he was acknowledged as sovereign of the entire kingdom, was to make provision for the public ordinances of religion for the benefit of the whole people. The Mosaic institutions were now for the first time carried into full effect, and permanently established. Many of the psalms, the most interesting and animating as well as the most instructive and edifying part of public worship, were composed during his reign, and in great part by himself. The knowledge of the divine law thus diffused among all ranks throughout the land, and the attractions given to the worship of the sanctuary, gradually and silently withdrew the people from the love and practice of idolatry.

It was less as a monarch than as a divinely inspired teacher of religious truth, that his influence was felt both in its immediate and its permanent results. It infused a new spirit into the nation, changed the tone of its poetic literature, and exerted a moulding and refining power over the national mind. These moral results of this influence have been happily expressed in the following lines :

> "It softened men of iron mould;
> It gave them virtues not their own.
> No ear so dull, no soul so cold,
> That felt not, fired not to the tone,
> Till David's lyre grew mightier than his throne."

Still there were elements of evil, which neither his royal power nor the influence of these divine truths could effectually control. These are the subject of frequent lamentation, sometimes of stern admonition and rebuke, and occasionally of severe denunciation. The wars so long waged for establishing his sovereignty, and extending it over the whole promised land, required a large military force, and concentrated in two successful military chieftains, the sons of Zeruiah, a power formidable to the monarch and oppressive to his people. The imperious temper of Joab, his use of every means for his own aggrandizement, and the tyranny which his success as a military leader enabled him to exercise over his sovereign, were among the severest trials of David's reign. The following examples will suffice for illustration.

When Abner proposed uniting the whole people under David's sovereignty, Joab foresaw the decline of his own popularity and power in the elevation which another would gain by so important a service to the throne. He boldly remonstrated with David for having given Abner a hearing, and then treacherously assassinated his rival.* (2 Sam. 3 : 17–27.) This traitorous act, though directed against his own kingly authority, David felt himself unable to punish. His own language, on this occasion, is an instructive comment on their relations throughout his reign. "I am this day weak, though anointed king ; and these men, the sons of Zeruiah, are too hard for me. The Lord shall reward the doer of evil, according to

* The sacred historian adds (vv. 27, 30) that it was "for the blood of Asahel his brother." This doubtless added fuel to his hate, and was probably the plea in justification of the deed; but Joab's own language shows that jealousy of a rival prompted the stroke.

his wickedness" (2 Sam. 3 : 39). The sentiment expressed in the last sentence will be found many times repeated in his psalms.

Joab's language to David, when overwhelmed with grief for the death of Absalom, shows how much he could presume upon the necessities of his king, and upon the obligations he was under to his servant. When told that the king wept and mourned for Absalom, thus turning the victory into mourning to all the people, he saw its unfavorable bearing upon himself, and the necessity of a change in the king's demeanor. "And Joab came into the house to the king, and said : Thou hast shamed this day the faces of all thy servants, who this day have saved thy life, and the lives of thy sons and of thy daughters. . . . Now therefore, arise, go forth, and speak comfortably to thy servants. For I swear by the Lord, if thou go not forth, there will not tarry one with thee this night ; and that will be worse to thee than all the evil that befell thee from thy youth until now." (2 Sam. 19 : 1–7.)

David now resolved to rid himself of this imperious servant, by putting Amasa in his place. His language to Amasa on this occasion was : "God do so to me and more also, if thou be not captain of the host before me continually in the room of Joab." (2 Sam. 19 : 13.) But again Joab thwarted his sovereign's purpose by treacherously slaying his rival ; and then, by heading the expedition for quelling the insurrection of Sheba, he recovered his former position, and made his services necessary to his sovereign. He was as politic as he was reckless, and understood the artifices by which he could link his own interests and destiny with those of his king. The body of the murdered Amasa he left exposed to view, as evidence that nothing more was to be expected from his rival, commanding one of his men to say to all who saw it, "He that favors Joab, and he that is for David, let him go after Joab ;" leaving them no alternative but adherence to himself, or desertion of their sovereign. (2 Sam. 20 : 11.)

Under an arbitrary and unscrupulous leader of a large military force, scattered over the kingdom, and such adherents as he would naturally attach to himself, there must have been frequent acts of oppression which the monarch himself had not the power to redress. He appealed to the Supreme Arbiter and Judge, and taught the wronged to invoke, and the wrong-doer to fear him. Thus he appeals in the 10th Psalm :

> Arise, Jehovah ; O God, lift up thy hand ;
> do not forget the lowly.
> Wherefore has the wicked contemned God,
> said in his heart : Thou wilt not require it ?

Thou hast seen ; for thou dost look upon trouble and sorrow,
to set them on thy hand.
To thee the wretched will commit it ;
the orphan's helper hast thou been.
Break the arm of the wicked ;
and the evil man, thou wilt search out his wickedness till
thou find no more.

The 5th Psalm, written soon after the last-mentioned outrage of this "bloody and deceitful man," contains in these words a distinct and very marked allusion to him. It is a type of humanity too often reappearing, in its general features, in the world's history ; and was worthy of commemoration, in language meant by the Holy Spirit as an admonition and warning, wherever the word of God should come.

In all his psalms David speaks as the "Anointed of God" (2 Sam. 23 : 1), and as representing in himself a divinely constituted sovereignty (Ps. 18 : 50). Hence the language of imprecation in his psalms is not to be regarded as that of personal denunciation.

§ 6.

Pilgrim Songs. (*Psalms of Degrees.*)

THERE is a collection of fifteen psalms (Pss. 120–134), each bearing the title, Pilgrim Song,—literally, Song of the Ascents, of the goings-up, namely, to the Holy City; compare Ps. 122 : 4, "whither the tribes go up." That they were selected for use on such occasions is the most obvious and natural explanation of the title.* It is no valid objection to this view, that many, perhaps most of them, were written with another design ; being selected from existing psalms as appropriate to this use, either for their direct reference to the peculiar circumstances of the pilgrims, and their allusions to the Holy City the object of the pilgrimage, or for their general tone of piety and devotion, appropriate to any religious occasion. The selection may have originated in the pilgrimages from Babylon to the Holy Land, at the close of the captivity ; compare Ezra 7 : 9 (literally, "the going-up from Babylon"). This would account for the adoption of such psalms as the first in the collection (Ps. 120), and others of similar import.

* Another explanation, namely, that the psalm was so called from its gradational structure, is unsatisfactory, only two or three at most having more than very slight traces of this peculiar form.

Three annual pilgrimages to the holy city were required by the law. "Three times in the year shall all thy males appear before Jehovah thy God, in the place which he shall choose." (Deut. 16 : 16 ; compare Ex. 23 : 14–17.) This was required only of males ; but pious women voluntarily accompanied them, as is recorded of Hannah (1 Sam. 1 : 7, "year by year, when she went up to the house of Jehovah"), and of Mary (Luke 2 : 41, 42).

These pilgrimages would naturally be made in large companies ; the people of the same neighborhood, and the different branches of the same family (as intimated in Luke 2 : 44), joining together for mutual assistance and protection. On the way, they encamped by night in the open fields. A religious character was given to their daily journeys, by the singing of appropriate hymns at morning and evening worship. How beautiful and pertinent, as they were journeying toward the mountains of Jerusalem (Ps. 125 : 2), were the sentiments and language of the 121st Psalm !

> I will lift my eyes unto the mountains ;
> from whence shall my help come ?
> My help is from Jehovah,
> who made heaven and earth.
> Let him not suffer thy foot to waver ;
> he that keeps thee, let him not slumber.
> Behold he will not slumber, and will not sleep,
> that keeps Israel.
> Jehovah is thy keeper ;
> Jehovah is thy shade on thy right hand.
> By day the sun shall not smite thee,
> nor the moon by night.
> Jehovah will keep thee from all evil ;
> he will keep thy soul.
> Jehovah will keep thy going out and thy coming in,
> henceforth and forevermore.

On the arrival of the pilgrims at the holy city, their joyful entrance through its gates was celebrated in the next following psalm (Ps. 122), beginning :

> I was glad when they said to me,
> let us go into the house of Jehovah.
> Our feet are standing
> in thy gates, O Jerusalem.

These two psalms are distinctive in their character and object, and indicate the design of the whole collection.

§ 7.

Poetic Form of the Psalms.

THE form of Hebrew poetry, as it appears in the Psalms, is very simple. It consists chiefly in a measured arrangement, or rhythmical proportion, of the members of a sentence, technically called parallelism. Its most perfect form is where two successive members of a sentence express the same, or nearly the same sense in different words, its charm being the felicitous, though slight, variation in expression of the same thought. For example :

Ps. 8 : 4. What is man, that thou shouldst be mindful of him,
and a son of man, that thou shouldst visit him?
Ps. 21 : 8. Thy hand shall find out all thy enemies ;
thy right hand shall find out those that hate thee.
Ps. 19 : 2. Day to day utters speech,
and night to night shows knowledge.

This is technically called the synonymous parallelism ; tne two members being composed of corresponding synonymous terms, called parallel terms; as in the first example, "man" in the first member and "a son of man" in the second, "be mindful of" in the first member and "visitest" in the second.

In this form the sense is usually completed in a single parallelism ; but it is sometimes continued through two or more, as in Ps. 89 : 30–33.

If his sons forsake my law,
and walk not in my judgments ;
if they profane my statutes,
and keep not my commandments ;
then will I visit their transgression with a rod,
and their iniquity with stripes ;
but my loving-kindness I will not withdraw from him,
and will not be false to my faith.

This form is too monotonous for very frequent use. Some variety is given to it in the following manner.

1. By inversion in the second member.

Ps. 91 : 14. For he has set his love upon me, and I will deliver him ;
I will set him on high, because he knows my name.

2. By repeating only a part of the first member in the second.

Ps. 8 : 3. When I behold thy heavens, the work of thy fingers,
moon and stars which thou hast ordained.
Ps. 96 : 3. Declare his glory among the nations,
his wonders among all the peoples.

There is another form of parallelism, in which the construction of the members is the same, or very similar, but with more or less variation of the sense: as in Ps. 19 : 7–11.

The law of Jehovah is perfect, converting the soul;
the testimony of Jehovah is sure, making wise the simple.
The statutes of Jehovah are right, rejoicing the heart;
the commandment of Jehovah is pure, enlightening the eyes.
The fear of Jehovah is clean, enduring forever;
the judgments of Jehovah are truth, they are righteous altogether;
more to be desired than gold, and much fine gold,
and sweeter than honey, and the dropping of the combs.
Moreover, by them is thy servant warned;
in keeping them there is great reward.

This is technically called the synthetic, or constructive, parallelism, and is varied like the preceding one.

In another form, the correspondence of the two members consists in an opposition of sentiment and of the parallel terms.

Ps. 20 : 8. They have bowed down and fallen;
but we are risen and stand upright.
Ps. 37 : 22. For they that are blessed of him shall inherit the land,
and they that are cursed of him shall be cut off.

This is technically called the antithetic parallelism. It is little used in the Psalms, but abounds in the Book of Proverbs, being well adapted to the expression of the thought in a large portion of that book.

There are also compound parallelisms consisting of three or more members; as in Ps. 1 : 1.

Happy the man,
who walks not in the counsel of the wicked,
nor stands in the way of sinners,
nor sits in the seat of scoffers.

A stanza of four members may consist of two simple parallelisms united in one sentence; as in Ps. 114 : 1, 2.

When Israel went forth out of Egypt,
the house of Jacob from a people of strange language,
Judah became his sanctuary,
Israel his dominion.

In such a stanza, the first member may correspond to the third, and the second to the fourth; as in Ps. 103 : 11, 12.

For as the heavens are high above the earth,
so great is his mercy toward them that fear him;
as far as the east is from the west,
so far has he removed our transgressions from us.

These are the most regular and perfect forms of parallelism. There are others less perfect, in which there is a less exact correspondence of the members in sense and grammatical construction, both being often continued from one member to the next, and even from one parallelism to another; as in Ps. 68 : 7, 8.

O God, when thou wentest forth before thy people,
  when thou didst march through the desert,
earth shook, yea the heavens dropped, at the presence of God,
  that Sinai, at the presence of God, the God of Israel.

The poetical form often differs from that of prose only by the division of the sentence into members of nearly equal length, having no special correspondence in sense or grammatical construction, a mere rhythmical parallelism; as in Ps. 115 : 1–8.

Not unto us, Jehovah, not unto us,
but to thy name, give glory.
Wherefore should the heathen say,
"where now is their God?"
But our God is in the heavens;
all that he pleased he has done.
Their idols are silver and gold,
the work of the hands of man.
A mouth have they, but they speak not;
eyes have they, but they see not;
ears have they, but they hear not;
a nose have they, but they smell not;
hands have they, but they handle not;
feet have they, but they walk not;
they make no sound in their throat.
Like them are they that made them,
all that trust in them.

But with these are interchanged the more regular and perfect forms, giving a higher poetical effect to the whole. It is the alternation of these numerous varieties in the forms of parallelism that constitutes the principal charm of the external form of Hebrew poetry.

§ 8.

Peculiarities of Structure.

1. The acrostic, or alphabetic form; in which the letters of the Hebrew alphabet, in their regular order, are the initial letters of the successive lines, or stanzas, of the poem. In the Psalms there are seven of this class; namely, Pss. 25, 34, 37, 111, 112, 119, 145. Pss. 111 and 112 are the simplest examples of this form, containing each the same number of lines as there are letters in the Hebrew alphabet, and the successive lines beginning with the letters in their regular order. These two psalms have another marked correspondence. In both, vv. 9 and 10 consist each of three members, the corresponding members in both psalms having the same initial letter, showing that the two were composed on the same plan. Ps. 119 is constructed with equal regularity, in twenty-two stanzas according to the number of the Hebrew letters, each stanza having eight parallelisms, or sixteen lines, and the first line of each parallelism beginning with the initial letter of the stanza. The memory was thus aided in treasuring up, and in calling to mind, the devout sentiments and practical precepts of the psalm. The remaining four, Pss. 25, 34, 37, 145, are not equally perfect, though nearly so.

2. Forms with a constantly recurring refrain after each member, as in Ps. 136.

3. The gradational form, where the closing sentiment or expression in the second member of each parallelism is repeated in the first member of the succeeding one; as in Ps. 121. Less perfect examples are found in Pss. 124 and 127.

4. The strophic form; as in Ps. 107, where vv. 8 and 9, 15 and 16, 21 and 22, 31 and 32, mark the division into strophes. Another example is found in Pss. 42 and 43, which evidently were written as one psalm, and in some manuscripts are united in one. The refrain in Ps. 42 : 5, 11, 43 : 5, divides it into three nearly equal parts. Ps. 57 is divided into two equal portions by the refrain in vv. 5 and 11. Ps. 80 is divided into four parts by the refrain in vv. 3, 7, 14 and 15 (varied in form), and 19.

5. Choral form, composed to be sung by alternating choirs; as Pss. 24, 115, 135.

That which distinguishes the poetry of the psalms, in its spirit, the essential and pervading characteristic, is religious sentiment. God, revealing himself in nature and his word as the Creator and Sovereign of the universe, as God of all the nations of the earth and in a special sense of his chosen people, these are the themes of the Hebrew poet, and the basis of all his religious and moral views and sentiments. Whatever is sublime or beautiful in nature is sung only in praise of its more glorious Author. The attributes of the Divine Being, the principles of his government, his purposes with regard to the destiny of man, his past, present, and prospective dealings with individuals and with nations, are here exhibited with all the resources of poetic art. Religious experience is delineated in its various forms, and under every condition and relation in life. But the national traits are everywhere preserved. All is domestic. The various fortunes of the Hebrew race, in its earlier history, furnished ample materials for historical illustration, whilst the gorgeous scenery of the Holy Land, its sublime mountains, its lovely hills and valleys, plains and rivers, and its romantic pastoral life, supplied inexhaustible stores of imagery from nature, for every purpose of poetic illustration and embellishment.

PSALMS.

FIRST BOOK.

PSALM I.

1 Happy the man,
Who walks not in the counsel of the wicked,
Nor stands in the way of sinners,
Nor sits in the seat of scoffers;
2 But in the law of Jehovah is his delight,
And in his law he meditates day and night.
3 And he shall be as a tree planted by the water-courses,
Which yields its fruit in its season;
And his leaf shall not wither,
And whatsoever he doeth shall prosper.
4 Not so are the wicked,
But as the chaff which the wind drives away.
5 Therefore the wicked shall not stand in the judgment,
Nor sinners in the congregation of the righteous.
6 For Jehovah knows the way of the righteous;
But the way of the wicked shall perish.

V. 3. Shall prosper.] *Or*, he will cause to prosper.

V. 6. Knows.] Recognizes, as that which he approves and delights in.

PSALM II.

1 WHY do the heathen rage,
And peoples imagine a vain thing,
2 The kings of the earth set themselves,
And rulers take counsel together,
Against Jehovah, and against his Anointed?
3 Let us break their bands asunder,
And cast away their cords from us.
4 He that sits in the heavens will laugh;
The Lord will deride them.
5 Then will he speak to them in his anger,
And will confound them in his hot displeasure:
6 Yet it is I that have anointed my king,
On Zion, my holy mount.
7 I will declare the decree.
Jehovah said to me: Thou art my Son;
I this day have begotten thee.
8 Ask of me,
And I will give the heathen for thine inheritance,
And the ends of the earth for thy possession.
9 Thou shalt break them with a rod of iron;
Thou shalt dash them in pieces like a potter's vessel.
10 Now then, ye kings, be wise;
Be warned, ye judges of the earth.
11 Serve Jehovah with fear;
And rejoice with trembling.
12 Kiss the Son, lest he be angry and ye perish in the way;
For quickly will his anger burn.
Happy are all who put their trust in him.

V. 3. The language of the rebel kings and rulers.

V. 6. Jehovah speaks.

VV. 7–9. The Anointed speaks.

V. 9. Rod.] *Or*, sceptre. For the sentiment, compare Is. 11 : 4; Rev. 19 : 15.

V. 12. Kiss the Son.] An expression either of homage to an anointed

PSALM III.

A Psalm of David, when he fled from Absalom his son.

1 JEHOVAH, how many are my foes!
Many are rising up against me.
2 Many are saying of my soul,
There is no salvation for him in God. (*Pause.*)
3 But thou, Jehovah, art a shield about me,
My glory, and he that lifts up my head.
4 With my voice I cry unto Jehovah,
And he hears me from his holy mount. (*Pause.*)
5 I have laid me down, and slept;
I have awaked; for Jehovah sustains me.
6 I will not be afraid of ten thousands of people,
Who have arrayed themselves against me round about.
7 Arise, Jehovah; save me, my God;
For thou hast smitten all my enemies on the cheek bone;
The teeth of the wicked thou hast broken.
8 The salvation is of Jehovah.
Thy blessing be upon thy people! (*Pause.*)

---

sovereign (compare 1 Sam. 10 : 1), or of submission and reconciliation. In the way.] In your course of resistance. *Or*, as to the way. Either, as to your course of conduct (compare Ps. 1 : 6, their "way — shall perish") or as to your lot, lest it be that ye perish.

Ps. iii. (title). When he fled.] For the history, see 2 Sam. chs. 15–18; and for the immediate occasion of the Psalm, ch. 17 : 1, 2, and 15–26. The fifth verse intimates that it was a morning hymn of praise, after passing the night in safety amid surrounding perils.

V. 2. Many are saying.] Whether adversaries, or desponding friends. Of my soul.] *Or*, to my soul (namely, so as deeply to affect me).

Pause.] The Hebrew word, unconnected with the text itself, probably means *rest, pause*, a musical term directing a suspension of the vocal performance, while the instrumental music was continued. But it marks, at the same time, a natural pause of thought after a sentiment of special interest and significance, as something to be dwelt upon; and in this use it is found even at the close of a Psalm. (Pss. iii., ix., xxix.) It is not to be read as a part of the text.

V. 7. Hast smitten.] In past times, and former seasons of peril.

PSALM IV.

To the chief Musician. With stringed instruments. A Psalm of David.

1 When I call, answer thou me, my righteous God!
In the distress thou didst give me enlargement;
Be gracious to me and hear my prayer.
2 Sons of men, how long shall my glory be for shame,
How long will ye love vanity, seek a lie? (*Pause.*)
3 But know that Jehovah has set apart his Beloved;
Jehovah will hear when I call to him.
4 Stand in awe, and do not sin;
Commune with your heart upon your bed,
And be still. (*Pause.*)
5 Offer sacrifices of righteousness,
And put your trust in Jehovah.
6 Many are saying: Who will cause us to see good?
Lift upon us the light of thy countenance, O Jehovah!

Ps. iv. (title). To the chief Musician.] Indicating the delivery of the Psalm to his care, for use in the religious service of the sanctuary.

With stringed instruments.] Denoting the kind of instrumental accompaniment. Compare the title to Ps. v. This Psalm seems to belong to the same occasion as the preceding one, but with some favorable change (v. 1, second line), as indicated in its calmer tone. V. 8 intimates that it was an evening hymn.

V. 2. My glory.] As in Ps. 3 : 3. Be for shame.] An object of contempt and scorn in the person of his representative. Vanity.] Vain, as being morally worthless and base, as well as unattainable. A lie.] False in itself (as is every evil object of pursuit) and certain to deceive.

V. 3. *Or*, has set apart a beloved one for himself. His Beloved.] Compare Ps. 18 : 19, "He delighted in me."

V. 4. *Or*, Say it (that is, consider it) in your heart.

V. 5. Sacrifices of righteousness.] Required by the divine law of righteousness; a right temper of heart being the essential element, of which the outward form was only an expression.

V. 6. Many are saying.] In the present disturbed condition of the State, and uncertainty of the future. Who will.] Implying despair of any source of relief. The Psalmist directs to the only true one.

7 Thou hast put gladness in my heart,
More than in the time when their corn and their new wine increased.
8 In peace will I both lay me down and sleep;
For thou Jehovah, alone,
Wilt make me dwell in safety.

PSALM V.

To the chief Musician. To the music of wind-instruments. A Psalm of David.

1 Give ear to my words, O Jehovah;
Consider my complaint.
2 Attend to the voice of my cry, my King, and my God;
For to thee will I pray.
3 Jehovah, in the morning shalt thou hear my voice;
In the morning will I direct [my prayer] to thee, and will watch.
4 For thou art not a God that has pleasure in wickedness;
Evil shall not dwell with thee.
5 The proud shall not stand in thy sight;
Thou hatest all workers of iniquity.
6 Thou wilt destroy them that speak falsehood;
Jehovah will abhor the bloody and deceitful man.
7 But I, in the abundance of thy kindness will I come into thy house;
I will worship toward thy holy temple, in thy fear.
8 Jehovah, lead me in thy righteousness because of my enemies;
Make plain thy way before me.

V. 7. More than.] More than they have in their prosperity.

Ps. v. belongs apparently to the same period as the two preceding ones, though subsequent to both, and when the royal fugitive was restored to his capital. (Compare v. 7.) V. 3 intimates that it was a morning hymn.

V. 3. Will watch.] For the answer, the looked-for help.

9 For there is nothing certain in their mouth;
Their inward part is corruption;
Their throat is an opened sepulchre;
They make smooth their tongue.
10 Let them bear their guilt, O God!
They shall fall by their own counsels.
In the multitude of their transgressions thrust them out;
For they have rebelled against thee.
11 But all that trust in thee shall rejoice;
They shall ever shout for joy, and thou wilt defend them;
And they that love thy name shall be joyful in thee.
12 For thou, Jehovah, wilt bless the righteous;
With favor, as with a shield, wilt thou encompass him.

PSALM VI.

To the chief Musician. With stringed instruments, upon the eighth. A Psalm of David.

1 JEHOVAH, do not in thine anger rebuke me,
And do not in thy hot displeasure correct me.
2 Be gracious to me, Jehovah, for I waste away;
Heal me, Jehovah, for my bones are shaken.
3 And my soul is sorely shaken;
And thou, Jehovah, how long!
4 Return, O Jehovah, deliver my soul;
Save me, for thy mercy's sake.

V. 9. Nothing certain in their mouth.] Nothing sure in their words, nothing that can be relied on and confided in.

V. 10. *Or*, shall fall from their counsels (shall fail of accomplishing them).

Ps. vi. (title). The eighth.] Of uncertain meaning; most probably, the lowest tone in the scale, and on which the instrument to be used was keyed.

The Psalm appears to have been composed in sickness, aggravated by the unkindness of enemies.

5 For in death there is no remembrance of thee;
In the underworld who will give thee thanks!
6 I am wearied with my groaning;
All the night I make my couch to swim,
With tears I cause my bed to flow.
7 Mine eye is wasted with grief,
Is grown old because of all my adversaries.
8 Depart from me all ye workers of iniquity;
For Jehovah has heard the voice of my weeping.
9 Jehovah has heard my supplication;
Jehovah will receive my prayer.
10 All my enemies shall be ashamed and sorely dismayed;
They shall turn back, shall be ashamed, suddenly.

PSALM VII.

A plaintive song of David, which he sang to Jehovah concerning the words of Cush, a Benjamite.

1 JEHOVAH, my God, in thee I put my trust;
Save me from all my persecutors, and deliver me;
2 Lest he tear my soul, like a lion,
Rending in pieces, and there be no deliverer!
3 Jehovah, my God, if I have done this,
If there is iniquity in my hands;

V. 5. That these words are to be taken in a qualified sense, is evident from Pss. 16 : 11 ; 17 : 15 ; 49 : 14, 15, and other clear views of the ultimate future, both of the righteous and the wicked.

Ps. vii. (title.) Cush, a Benjamite.] Not otherwise known; probably one of the court of Saul (being of the same tribe, compare 1 Sam. 22 : 7) when David was the object of his persecutions, and of the malicious calumnies of those around him. See 1 Sam. chs. 18–28 ; especially 18 : 9–29 ; 19 : 9–24 ; 23 : 7–15, and 19–26.

V. 2. Lest he.] Saul; from whom, of all the enemies just spoken of, there was most to fear.

V. 3. Have done this.] Referring to the charge contained in "the words of Cush," of which there is no record.

4 If I have requited with evil him that was at peace with
me,—
Yea, I have delivered him that without cause oppressed
me;—
5 Then let the enemy pursue my soul, and overtake it,
And tread down my life to the earth,
And lay my honor in the dust. (*Pause.*)
6 Arise, O Jehovah, in thine anger;
Raise thyself up amid the wrath of my adversaries,
And awake for me; thou hast commanded judgment.
7 And let the assembly of the peoples encompass thee round,
And return to the place on high, above them.
8 Jehovah will judge the nations;
Judge me, O Jehovah,
According to my righteousness, and according to my integrity within me.
9 Let now the evil of the wicked come to an end;
And thou wilt establish the just,
Even trying the hearts and reins,
Righteous God!
10 My shield is with God,
Who saves the upright in heart.
11 God is a righteous judge;
And God is angry every day.
12 If one turn not, he will whet his sword;
His bow he has bent, and made it ready,
13 And has aimed at him weapons of death;
His arrows he will make burning ones.
14 Behold, he will travail with iniquity,
And conceive mischief, and bring forth falsehood.

V. 4. I have delivered.] See 1 Sam. 24 : 4–7 ; 26 : 8–12.

V. 7. And return.] Resume the place of judgment, above the assembled throngs.

V. 8. Judge me.] Act as my judge, for my vindication. Within me.] *Or*, over me (as a protection).

V. 11. *Or*, God judges the righteous.

15 He digged a pit, and hollowed it out,
And fell into the ditch he made.
16 His mischief will return upon his own head,
And upon his crown will his violence descend.
17 I will praise Jehovah, according to his righteousness,
And will sing praise to the name of Jehovah Most High.

PSALM VIII.

To the chief Musician. On the Gittith. A Psalm of David.

1 JEHOVAH, our Lord,
How excellent is thy name in all the earth;
Thou whose glory is set upon the heavens!
2 Out of the mouth of children and nurslings hast thou founded strength,
Because of thine adversaries,
To silence the enemy and the revenger.
3 When I behold thy heavens, the work of thy fingers,
Moon and stars which thou hast ordained;
4 What is man, that thou shouldst be mindful of him,
And a son of man, that thou shouldst visit him;
5 And shouldst make him little lower than angels,
And shouldst crown him with glory and honor;
6 Shouldst give him dominion over the works of thy hands!
All thou hast put under his feet;
7 Sheep and oxen, all of them;
Yea, and beasts of the field,

Ps. viii. (title.) Gittith.] An instrument of music, to which three psalms (viii., lxxxi., lxxxiv.,) are directed to be sung. *Or*, After the Gittith (after the melody of that name).

V. 1. Whose glory is set upon the heavens.] Compare Ps. 19 : 1, "The heavens declare the glory of God."

V. 2. Founded strength.] Inspiring confidence to resist and quell the assaults of the enemy.

V. 5. *Or*, little lower than Deity.

8 Bird of heaven, and fishes of the sea,—
That which passes through paths of the seas.
9 Jehovah, our Lord,
How excellent is thy name in all the earth!

PSALM IX.

To the chief Musician. After [the melody] "Death of the Son." A Psalm of David.

1 I WILL praise Jehovah with my whole heart;
I will recount all thy wondrous works.
2 I will be glad and rejoice in thee,
I will sing praise to thy name, Most High,
3 When my enemies turn backward,
Stumble, and perish before thee.
4 For thou hast maintained my right and my cause;
Thou sattest in the throne, judging right.
5 Thou hast rebuked the heathen, hast destroyed the wicked;
Their name thou hast blotted out forever and ever.
6 As for the enemy, the desolations are ended forever;
And cities hast thou destroyed; their memory, even theirs, is perished.
7 But Jehovah will sit forever;
He has founded his throne for judgment.
8 And he will judge the habitable earth in righteousness;
He will judge peoples in uprightness.
9 So let Jehovah be a refuge for the oppressed,
A refuge in times of distress;

Ps. ix. (title.) Death of the Son.] A composition which gave the name to a melody to which this Psalm was to be sung. For the occasion (see v. 6), compare 2 Sam. 8 : 1–14.

V. 6. The desolations.] Of invading heathen armies; or (as the words may mean) the desolations inflicted on the enemy, so complete as to be ended forever, leaving nothing to be done. Even theirs.] Mighty and renowned as they were.

V. 8. The habitable earth.] Wherever men dwell.

10 And they will trust in thee who know thy name,
For thou hast not forsaken them that seek thee, Jehovah.
11 Sing praise to Jehovah, who dwells in Zion;
Make known his deeds among the peoples;
12 That he who makes inquisition for blood has remembered them,
Has not forgotten the cry of the suffering.
13 Be gracious to me, Jehovah;
Behold my suffering from them that hate me,
Thou that liftest me up from the gates of death;
14 That I may recount all thy praise,
In the gates of the daughter of Zion,—
May exult in thy salvation.
15 The heathen have sunk down in the pit they made;
In the net which they hid is their own foot taken.
16 Jehovah made himself known; he executed judgment;
In the work of his hands was the wicked snared. (*Music Pause.*)
17 The wicked shall turn back, to the underworld,
All the heathen that forget God.
18 For the needy shall not always be forgotten;
The hope of the humble shall not perish forever.
19 Arise, Jehovah! Let not man prevail;
Let the heathen be judged before thee.
20 Put them in fear, O Jehovah;
Let the heathen know that they are men. (*Pause.*)

PSALM X.

1 Wherefore, O Jehovah, standest thou afar off,
Hidest thyself in times of distress?
2 The wicked in his pride persecutes the lowly;
Let them be taken in the devices which they contrived.
3 For the wicked glories in his soul's desire,
And greedy of gain forsakes, contemns Jehovah.

4 The wicked, through his pride of countenance, will not seek;
God is not in all his thoughts.
5 His ways are sure at all times;
Thy judgments are far above, out of his sight;
As for all his adversaries, he scoffs at them.
6 He has said in his heart: I shall not be moved;
I shall never be in adversity.
7 With cursing is his mouth filled, and with deceits and extortion;
Under his tongue is mischief and falsehood.
8 He sits in ambush by the villages;
In the secret places he slays the innocent;
His eyes lurk for the wretched.
9 He lies in wait in the hiding place as a lion in his covert;
He lies in wait to seize upon the weak;
He seizes upon the weak when he has drawn him into his net.
10 He bows himself, he crouches down,
And the wretched fall by his strong ones.
11 He says in his heart: God has forgotten;
He has hidden his face, he sees it not forever.
12 Arise, Jehovah; O God, lift up thy hand;
Do not forget the lowly.
13 Wherefore has the wicked contemned God,
Said in his heart: Thou wilt not require it?

V. 4. Will not seek.] Is too proud and self-confident to look beyond himself for help, or (second member) to acknowledge a God. The words may be rendered (perhaps more pertinently, in the connection):

The wicked, according to his pride of countenance, "He will not require it,"
"There is no God,"—are all his thoughts.

Require.] Compare the use of this word in Gen. 9 : 5.

V. 5. Thy judgments.] The divine purpose in the infliction of judgments is far above his earthly and sensual views.

V. 12. The lowly.] The humble in condition; and helpless (except through the help of God) against the oppression of the strong.

14 Thou hast seen; for thou dost look upon trouble and
sorrow,
To set them on thy hand.
To thee the wretched will commit it;
The orphan's helper hast thou been.
15 Break the arm of the wicked;
And the evil man, thou wilt search out his wickedness till
thou find no more.
16 Jehovah is king forever;
The heathen have perished from his land.
17 The desire of the lowly thou hast heard, O Jehovah;
Thou wilt confirm their heart, thou wilt incline thine ear.
18 To judge the orphan and oppressed,
That he no more may dread man that is of the earth.

PSALM XI.

To the chief Musician. [A Psalm] of David.

1 In Jehovah put I my trust.
How say ye to my soul:
Flee [as] a bird to your mountain!
2 For lo, the wicked bend the bow;
They have fitted their arrow upon the string,
To shoot covertly at the upright in heart.
3 When the foundations are destroyed,
What can the righteous do?

V. 14. On thy hand.] Where they are ever before him. Compare Is. 49 : 16.

V. 18. *Or*, that man, that is of the earth, may put in fear no more.

Ps. xi. The sentiments of the Psalm point clearly to the period of the persecution of David by Saul and his adherents, 2 Sam. 18–30. Compare especially 28 : 7–26.

V. 3. Foundations.] Namely, of social order, on which the peace and security of society rest. The language is applicable to the whole reign of Saul.

4 Jehovah is in his holy temple ;
Jehovah,—in heaven is his throne.
His eyes behold,
His eyelids try, the sons of men.
5 Jehovah tries the righteous ;
And the wicked, and lover of violence, his soul hates.
6 He will rain on the wicked snares,
Fire and brimstone, and a burning tempest,—
The portion of their cup !
7 For righteous is Jehovah, he loves righteousness ;
His countenance beholds the upright.

PSALM XII.

To the chief Musician. On the eighth. A Psalm of David.

1 SAVE, Jehovah, for the godly ceases ;
For the faithful fail from the sons of men.
2 They speak falsehood every man with his neighbor ;
With flattering lips, with a double heart, they speak.
3 May Jehovah cut off all flattering lips,
The tongue that speaks proud things ;
4 Who say : With our tongue will we prevail ;
Our lips are our own ; who is lord over us ?
5 For the oppression of the lowly, for the sighing of the needy,
Now will I arise, saith Jehovah ;
I will set him in safety at whom he scoffs.

V. 4. Temple.] Compare 1 Sam. 1 : 9 ; 3 : 3 ; showing that the tabernacle, which contained the ark, the symbol of Jehovah's presence, was so called.

V. 5. Tries the righteous.] With the implication that he finds him faithful ; as must be the result of such a trial.

Ps. xii. (title.) On the eighth.] See Ps. vi.

V. 5. *Or*, I will set him in safety who pants for it.

6 The sayings of Jehovah are pure sayings ;
Silver tried in a furnace of earth,
Seven times refined.
7 Thou, Jehovah, wilt keep them,
Wilt guard them from this generation forever.
8 The wicked walk on every side,
When the vilest of the sons of men are exalted.

PSALM XIII.

To the chief Musician. A Psalm of David.

1 How long, Jehovah! Wilt thou forget me forever?
How long wilt thou hide thy face from me?
2 How long shall I take counsel in my soul,
[Bear] sorrow in my heart, daily?
How long shall my enemy be exalted over me?
3 Look, I pray, answer me, Jehovah, my God ;
Lighten mine eyes, lest I sleep the [sleep of] death ;
4 Lest my enemy say : I have prevailed over him ;
Lest my foes exult when I am ready to fall.
5 But I, in thy kindness have I trusted ;
Let my heart exult in thy salvation.
6 I will sing to Jehovah, for he has been bountiful to me.

PSALM XIV.

To the chief Musician. [A Psalm] of David.

1 The fool has said in his heart: There is no God.
Corrupt, abominable are they in their works ;
There is none that doeth good.

V. 6. *Or*, silver melted to the ground in a furnace. Meaning : melted from the ore in a furnace, and flowing down to the ground,—to the receptacle in the earth.

2 Jehovah looked down from heaven upon the sons of men,
To see if there is any that understands,
That seeks after God.
3 They have all turned aside ; together they are corrupted ;
There is none that doeth good, not even one.
4 Have all the workers of iniquity no knowledge,
Who eat up my people as they eat bread,
Call not upon Jehovah ?
5 There were they in great fear ;
For God is in the righteous generation.
6 Ye put to shame the counsel of the lowly,
For Jehovah is his refuge.
7 Oh for the salvation of Israel out of Zion!
When Jehovah turns the captivity of his people,
Jacob will exult, Israel will rejoice.

PSALM XV.

A Psalm of David.

1 JEHOVAH, who shall sojourn in thy tabernacle?
Who shall dwell in thy holy mount?
2 He that walks uprightly, and works righteousness,
And speaks truth in his heart.
3 He has not slandered with his tongue,
Has not done evil to his fellow,
Nor taken up a reproach against his neighbor.
4 In his eyes a reprobate is abhorred ;
But he will honor them that fear Jehovah.
If he has sworn to his harm, he will not change.

V. 6. By "counsel of the lowly" is meant whatever he devises, or resorts to, for security. As his reliance is on the righteous sovereignty of God, whoever wrongs him "puts it to shame."

V. 7. Turns the captivity.] A proverbial phrase, meaning restoration to prosperity. See the remark on Ps. 85 : 1.

V. 1. Sojourn in thy tabernacle.] Meaning, to frequent it, to be as it were Jehovah's guest, and under his care and protection.

5 His money he has not put out at usury;
Nor has he taken a bribe against the innocent.
He that does these things shall never be moved.

PSALM XVI.

Memorial [Psalm] of David.

1 PRESERVE me, O God, for I trust in thee.
2 Thou [my soul] hast said to Jehovah: Thou art Lord;
My good is not aside from thee.
3 As for the saints who are in the earth,
[They are] the excellent, in whom is all my delight.
4 Their sorrows shall be multiplied that exchange for another.
I will not pour out their drink-offerings of blood,
And will not take their names upon my lips.
5 Jehovah is the portion of my heritage and of my cup;
Thou wilt maintain my lot.
6 The lines have fallen to me in pleasant places;
Yea, I have a goodly heritage.
7 I will bless Jehovah who has counseled me;
Also by night my reins admonish me.
8 I have set Jehovah always before me;
Because [he is] on my right hand, I shall not be moved.
9 Therefore my heart is glad, and my glory exults;
Also my flesh shall rest in hope.

V. 2. Thou [my soul] hast said.] Appealing to his self-consciousness of this truth, as though strengthening himself in the conviction of it, as his sole reliance in the hour of trial. "Soul" is implied in the form of the Hebrew verb.

V. 4. Another.] Compare Is. 48 : 11, "I will not give my glory to another." Another god, is the implication in both passages.

V. 6. Lines.] Measuring lines, by which lands were measured off for division. Compare Ps. 78 : 55, "divided them a heritage by line."

V. 7. Admonish me.] Namely, of this duty, to bless Jehovah.

V. 9. My glory.] The distinguishing and nobler part of man, his spiritual in distinction from his material, physical nature.

10 For thou wilt not abandon my soul to the underworld;
Thou wilt not suffer thy Holy One to see corruption.
11 Thou wilt show me the path of life,
Fullness of joys in thy presence,
Pleasures at thy right hand, for evermore!

PSALM XVII.

A Prayer of David.

1 HEAR, O Jehovah, the right;
Be attentive to my cry.
Give ear to my prayer,
From lips not deceitful.
2 Let my sentence come forth from thy presence;
Let thine eyes behold the things that are equal.
3 Thou hast tried my heart, hast visited by night,
Hast assayed me,—thou findest nothing.
I have purposed, my mouth shall not transgress.
4 As to the deeds of man, by the word of thy lips
I have kept myself from the paths of the violent.
5 My steps have held fast to thy ways;
My feet have not wavered.
6 I have called upon thee, for thou wilt answer me, O God;
Incline thine ear to me, hear my speech.
7 Show thy marvelous kindness, thou that savest the trusting,
From such as rise up against them, with thy right hand.
8 Keep me as the apple of the eye;
In the shadow of thy wings thou wilt hide me,
9 From the wicked that oppress me,
My deadly enemies that encompass me round.
10 They are inclosed in their own fat;
With their mouth they speak proudly.

V. 10. Holy One.] *Or*, Beloved; compare Ps. 4 : 3.

V. 9. *Or*, my enemies that eagerly encompass me round.

V. 10. In their own fat.] An expression either of luxurious ease, or

11 At our footsteps they have now encompassed us;
They have set their eyes to bow [us] down to the earth.
12 He is like a lion that is greedy for prey,
And as a young lion lurking in secret places.
13 Arise, O Jehovah!
Confront him; make him crouch down.
Deliver my soul from the wicked, thy sword,
14 From men, thy hand, Jehovah;
From men of the world, whose portion is in life,
And with thy hoard thou wilt fill their belly.
They shall be surfeited with sons,
And leave their excess to their children.
15 As for me, in righteousness shall I behold thy face,
Shall be satisfied, when I awake, with thy likeness.

PSALM XVIII.

To the chief Musician. By the servant of Jehovah, by David, who spoke to Jehovah the words of this song, in the day when Jehovah had delivered him from the hand of all his enemies, and from the hand of Saul; and he said:

1 I WILL love thee, Jehovah, my strength.
2 Jehovah is my rock, and my fortress, and my deliverer,
My God, my rock, I will trust in him;
My shield, my horn of salvation, my high tower.
3 Praised will I call Jehovah,
And from my enemies shall I be saved.

---

of grossness in regard to spiritual perception. For the former, compare Job 15 : 27; and for the latter, Is. 6 : 10.

V. 11. They have set their eyes.] Namely, on this object; they are wholly intent on it. Compare the similar expression in Luke 9 : 53.

V. 15. With thy likeness.] With God, as manifested to those whom he permits to behold him. Compare Matt. 5 : 8.

V. 2 Horn, emblem of strength and of defense; of salvation, as the instrument and means of it.

4 The bands of death encompassed me,
And floods of the ungodly made me afraid.
5 The bands of the underworld surrounded me,
The snares of death confronted me.
6 In my distress I called upon Jehovah,
And unto my God I cried.
From his temple he heard my voice,
And my cry came before him, into his ears.
7 Then the earth shook and quaked;
And the foundations of the mountains trembled,
And were shaken, because he was wroth.
8 There went up smoke in his nostril,
And fire out of his mouth devoured;
Coals were kindled from it.
9 And he bowed the heavens and came down,
And thick darkness was under his feet.
10 And he rode upon a cherub, and did fly,
And soared along on wings of the wind.
11 He made darkness his covering,
His pavilion round about him;
Dark waters, thick clouds of the skies.
12 From the brightness before him his thick clouds passed away;
Hail, and coals of fire!
13 And Jehovah thundered in the heavens,
And the Most High uttered his voice;
Hail, and coals of fire!
14 And he sent out his arrows and scattered them,
And shot forth lightnings and discomfited them.
15 And the channels of water were seen,
And the foundations of the world were made bare,
At thy rebuke, O Jehovah,
At the blast of the breath of thy nostrils.

V. 12. The scene now changes. A blaze of light, from before him, disperses the darkness of enveloping clouds, in showers of hail and burning coals.

VV. 12, 13. Hail and coals of fire.] Compare Ex. 9 : 23, 24.

16 He sent from on high, he took me,
He drew me out of many waters.
17 He delivered me from my strong enemy,
And from them that hated me, for they were too strong for me.
18 They confronted me in the day of my calamity;
And Jehovah became a stay for me,
19 And brought me forth to a large place,
And delivered me, because he delighted in me.
20 Jehovah requited me according to my righteousness;
According to the cleanness of my hands he recompensed me.
21 For I have kept the ways of Jehovah,
And have not wickedly departed from my God.
22 For all his judgments were before me,
And his statutes I put not away from me;
23 And I was upright with him,
And kept myself from my iniquity;
24 And Jehovah recompensed me according to my righteousness,
According to the cleanness of my hands before his eyes.
25 With the gracious thou wilt show thyself gracious;
With an upright man thou wilt show thyself upright;
26 With the pure thou wilt show thyself pure;
And with the froward thou wilt show thyself froward.
27 For thou wilt save an afflicted people,
And lofty eyes thou wilt bring low.
28 For thou wilt light my lamp;
Jehovah my God will enlighten my darkness.
29 For by thee I shall run through a troop,
And by my God I shall leap over a wall.
30 As for God, his way is perfect;
The word of Jehovah is tried;
A shield is he to all that trust in him.
31 For who is God besides Jehovah,
And who is a rock save our God;
32 The Mighty, that girds me with strength,
And has made my way perfect;

33 Making my feet like hinds',
And on my high places he makes me stand;
34 Teaching my hands to war,
And a bow of brass is bent by my arms.
35 And thou gavest me the shield of thy salvation;
And thy right hand will hold me up,
And thy condescension will make me great.
36 Thou wilt enlarge my steps under me,
And my ankles waver not.
37 I shall pursue my enemies, and overtake them;
And shall not turn again till they are consumed.
38 I shall smite them, and they will not be able to rise;
They will fall beneath my feet.
39 For thou hast girded me with strength for the battle;
Thou wilt make them crouch under me that rise up against me.
40 And thou hast given me the neck of my enemies;
And those that hate me, I will destroy them.
41 They will cry, and there is no deliverer;
To Jehovah, and he answers them not.
42 And I shall beat them small as dust before the wind;
As mire of the streets I will pour them out.
43 Thou wilt deliver me from the strifes of the people;
Thou wilt make me the head of the heathen;
A people I have not known shall serve me.
44 At the hearing of the ear they will obey me;
Strangers will profess submission to me.
45 Strangers will fade away,
And will tremble from their strongholds.
46 Jehovah lives, and blessed be my rock,
And let the God of my salvation be exalted;
47 The Mighty, who avenges me,
And has subdued peoples under me,
48 Delivering me from my enemies.
Yea, thou wilt lift me above those that rise up against me;
From the man of violence thou wilt rescue me.

V. 36. Waver not.] My feet stand firm, having ample room.

49 Therefore will I praise thee, Jehovah, among the heathen,
And to thy name will I sing.
50 Great deliverances he gives to his king,
And shows kindness to his anointed,
To David, and to his seed, forevermore.

PSALM XIX.

To the chief Musician. [A Psalm] of David.

1 THE heavens declare the glory of God,
And the expanse proclaims his handiwork.
2 Day to day utters speech,
And night to night shows knowledge.
3 There is no speech nor language,
Where their voice is not heard.
4 Their line is gone out through all the earth,
And their words to the end of the world.
In them has he set a tabernacle for the sun;
5 And he is as a bridegroom coming out of his chamber;
He rejoices as a strong man to run a race.
6 His going forth is from the end of the heavens,

V. 50. To his anointed—to David, and to his seed.] These words are the key to the sentiments of this psalm, and of all of like import. The Psalmist speaks as the representative of that divinely constituted sovereignty, of which he was the head, and which was opposed in his person.

V. 3. In every land, is meant. *Their* voice is heard, whatever may be the "speech or language" of the people. They preach to all, of every tongue, and are understood by all. The verse may be rendered thus:

There is no speech, there are no words;
Their voice is not heard.

This is true in itself, but has no special significance in the connection. The thought expressed in the text is both true and to the point. They declare the "glory of God and his handiwork" to all, in a voice that is heard by all. The italics of the common English version are not required by the Hebrew construction.

And his circuit unto the ends thereof,
And there is nothing hidden from his heat.
7 The law of Jehovah is perfect, converting the soul;
The testimony of Jehovah is sure, making wise the simple.
8 The precepts of Jehovah are right, rejoicing the heart;
The commandment of Jehovah is pure, enlightening the eyes.
9 The fear of Jehovah is clean, enduring forever;
The judgments of Jehovah are truth, they are righteous altogether;
10 More to be desired than gold, and much fine gold,
And sweeter than honey, and the dropping of the combs.
11 Moreover, by them is thy servant warned;
In keeping them there is great reward.
12 Errors, who can understand!
Of hidden ones do thou acquit me.
13 Also from presumptuous ones withhold thy servant;
Let them not have dominion over me;
Then shall I be upright, and be free from great transgression.
14 Let the words of my mouth, and meditation of my heart,
Be acceptable in thy sight,
Jehovah, my rock, and my redeemer.

PSALM XX.

To the chief Musician. A Psalm of David.

1 JEHOVAH answer thee in the day of trouble,
The name of the God of Jacob defend thee;
2 Send thee help from the sanctuary,
And strengthen thee from Zion;
3 Remember all thy offerings,
And accept thy burnt-sacrifice;

V. 12. Hidden ones.] Such as are unobserved, and of which one is not conscious, in distinction from deliberate and purposed sins, spoken of in the next verse.

4 Grant thee according to thy heart,
And fulfill all thy counsel.
5 May we shout for joy in thy deliverance,
And in the name of our God lift up a banner.
Jehovah fulfill all thy petitions.
6 Now know I,
That Jehovah saves his anointed.
He will answer him from his holy heavens,
With the saving strength of his right hand.
7 Some in chariots, and some in horses,
But we in the name of Jehovah our God, will glory.
8 They have bowed down and fallen;
But we are risen and stand upright.
9 Jehovah, save!
Let the king answer us, in the day we call.

PSALM XXI.

To the chief Musician. A Psalm of David.

1 JEHOVAH, in thy strength shall the king rejoice;
And in thy salvation how greatly shall he exult!
2 Thou hast given him his heart's desire,
And hast not withholden the request of his lips. (*Pause.*)
3 For thou dost anticipate him with blessings of goodness,
Thou settest a crown of pure gold on his head.
4 He asked of thee life, and thou gavest it to him,
Length of days forever and ever.
5 Great is his glory in thy salvation;
Honor and majesty thou dost lay upon him.
6 For thou makest him a blessing forever;
Thou dost gladden him with joy by thy countenance.
7 For the king trusts in Jehovah,

V. 6. More literally: Thou makest him blessings; referring to their variety and fullness. Compare Gen. 12 : 2, last clause.

And through the kindness of the Most High he shall not be moved.

8 Thy hand will find out all thy enemies ;
Thy right hand will find out those that hate thee.
9 Thou wilt make them as a fiery furnace in the time of thine anger ;
Jehovah will swallow them up in his wrath, and fire will devour them.
10 Their fruit thou wilt destroy from the earth,
And their seed from the sons of men.
11 For they spread out evil against thee ;
They devised a plot ; they shall not prevail.
12 For thou wilt make them turn their back ;
With thy bowstrings thou wilt aim against their face,
13 Exalt thyself, Jehovah, in thy strength ;
We will sing and praise in song thy power.

PSALM XXII.

To the chief Musician. After [the melody] " Hind of the Morning."
A Psalm of David.

1 My God, my God, why hast thou forsaken me !
Far from my deliverance are the words of my groaning.
2 My God, I cry, in the day-time, and thou answerest not ;
And in the night season, and there is no quiet for me.
3 But thou art holy,
Enthroned in the praises of Israel.
4 In thee our fathers trusted ;
They trusted, and thou didst deliver them.
5 To thee they cried, and were freed ;
In thee they trusted, and were not ashamed.

V. 9. The second member shows that the earthly sovereign is only the instrument of divine justice. Compare the note at the close of Ps. xviii.

V. 11. They spread out evil.] As a net is spread for the unwary.

V. 5. See Exodus 3 : 9, 10.

6 But I am a worm, and not a man;
A reproach of men, and despised of the people.
7 All that see me mock at me;
They thrust out the lip, they shake the head [saying]:
8 Commit it to Jehovah, he will deliver him;
He will rescue him, for he delights in him.
9 But thou art he that took me out of the womb,
That made me trust, when on my mother's breasts.
10 On thee was I cast from the womb;
From the bowels of my mother thou art my God.
11 Be not far from me, for trouble is near,
For there is no helper.
12 Many bulls have encompassed me;
Strong ones of Bashan have beset me round.
13 They gaped upon me with their mouth,
A ravening and roaring lion.
14 I am poured out like water,
And all my bones are parted.
My heart is become like wax;
Melted in the midst of my bowels.
15 My strength is dried up like a potsherd,
And my tongue cleaves to my jaws;
And thou wilt lay me in the dust of death.
16 For dogs have encompassed me;
The assembly of evil-doers have inclosed me,
Piercing my hands and my feet.
17 I may number all my bones;
They look, they stare upon me.
18 They part my garments among them,
And for my vesture they cast lots.
19 But thou, Jehovah, be not afar off;
O my strength, hasten to my help.
20 Rescue my soul from the sword,
My life from the power of the dog.

V. 8. Said ironically, and in bitter mockery of the Psalmist's trust in Jehovah. Compare Matt. 27 : 43.

V. 13. They.] The adversaries, here compared to a hungry lion.

21 Save me from the lion's mouth,
And answer [and rescue] me from the horns of wild oxen.
22 I will declare thy name to my brethren;
In the midst of the assembly will I praise thee.
23 Ye that fear Jehovah praise him;
All ye seed of Jacob glorify him,
And fear him all ye seed of Israel.
24 For he has not despised, nor abhorred, the affliction of the afflicted,
And has not hid his face from him;
And when he cried to him, he heard.
25 Of thee shall be my praise, in the great congregation;
My vows I will pay before them that fear him.
26 The humble shall eat, and shall be satisfied;
They will praise Jehovah that seek him;
May your heart live forever!
27 All the ends of the earth shall remember and turn to Jehovah,
And all the families of nations shall worship before thee.
28 For the kingdom is Jehovah's,
And he is ruler among the nations.
29 They eat and worship, all the rich of the earth;
Before him shall bow all that go down to the dust,
And he that can not keep his soul alive.
30 A seed shall serve him;
It shall be told of the Lord for generations.

V. 21. Wild oxen.] Described in Job 39 : 9–12, as peculiarly fierce and intractable.

V. 25. Of thee.] *Or*, from thee, as the source of my deliverance, and therefore of my praise.

V. 26. Shall eat.] Of the sacrificial feast made on occasion of the fulfillment of a vow (preceding verse). See Deut. 12 : 17, 18, Lev. 7 : 16; and compare an abuse of this religious observance, in Prov. 7 : 14.

V. 27. Shall remember.] The deliverance here commemorated.

V. 29. There is here no distinction of rank or condition. The feast is for all; for the rich, for "all that go down to the dust" (the common lot), for the poor, even such as "can not keep his soul alive."

31 They shall come, and shall make known his righteousness,
To a people that shall be born, that he has done it.

PSALM XXIII.

A Psalm of David.

1 JEHOVAH is my shepherd, I shall not want.
2 He makes me lie down in green pastures;
He leads me beside the still waters.
3 He restores my soul;
He guides me in paths of righteousness, for his name's sake.
4 Yea, though I walk through the valley of the shadow of death,
I will fear no evil, for thou art with me;
Thy rod and thy staff they comfort me.
5 Thou preparest a table before me, in the presence of my adversaries;
Thou anointest my head with oil; my cup runs over.
6 Surely goodness and mercy will follow me all the days of my life,
And I shall dwell in the house of Jehovah forever.

PSALM XXIV.

A Psalm of David.

1 THE earth is Jehovah's, and the fullness thereof;
The world and they that dwell therein.
2 For he founded it upon the seas,
And established it upon the floods.

Psalm xxiv. The most probable occasion of this psalm is the solemn procession, described in 1 Chron. 15 : 14–28, for the induction of the ark into the sanctuary prepared for it. It is not improbable that the psalm was chanted antiphonally, as in the division by paragraphs.

3 Who shall ascend into the mount of Jehovah,
And who shall stand in his holy place?
4 He that has clean hands, and a pure heart;
Who has not lifted up his soul to vanity,
And has not sworn deceitfully.
5 He shall receive a blessing from Jehovah,
And righteousness from the God of his salvation.
6 This is the generation of them that seek him,
That seek thy face, even Jacob. (*Pause.*)
7 Lift up your heads, ye gates,
And lift yourselves up, ye everlasting doors,
That the King of glory may come in.
8 Who is this, the King of glory?
Jehovah, strong and mighty;
Jehovah, mighty in battle.
9 Lift up your heads, ye gates,
And lift up, ye everlasting doors,
That the King of glory may come in.
10 Who then is he, the King of glory?
Jehovah of hosts;
He is the King of glory. (*Pause.*)

PSALM XXV.

[A Psalm] of David.

1 To thee, O Jehovah, I will lift up my soul.
2 My God, in thee do I trust; let me not be ashamed,
Let not my enemies triumph over me.
3 Yea, let none that wait for thee be ashamed;
Let them be ashamed that transgress without cause.
4 Make me know thy ways, O Jehovah;
Teach me thy paths.

V. 6. Jacob.] Used here, as elsewhere, for the true Israel, the collective people of God. Compare Ps. 14 : 7.

5 Make me walk in thy truth, and teach me;
For thou art the God of my salvation,
On thee I wait all the day.
6 Remember thy tender mercies, O Jehovah, and thy kindnesses;
For they have been of old.
7 The sins of my youth, and my trespasses, do not remember;
According to thy kindness remember thou me,
For thy goodness' sake, O Jehovah.
8 Good and upright is Jehovah;
Therefore will he direct sinners in the way.
9 He will guide the humble in that which is right,
And the humble he will teach his way.
10 All the paths of Jehovah are kindness and truth,
To such as keep his covenant and his testimonies.
11 For thy name's sake, O Jehovah,
Thou wilt pardon my iniquity, for it is great!
12 What man is he that fears Jehovah?
Him will he instruct in the way he should choose.
13 His soul shall dwell at ease,
And his seed shall possess the land.
14 The secret of Jehovah is for them that fear him,
And he makes them know his covenant.
15 Mine eyes are ever toward Jehovah;
For he will bring out my feet from the net.
16 Turn unto me, and be gracious to me;
For I am desolate and afflicted.
17 The troubles of my heart are enlarged;
Bring thou me out of my distresses.
18 Look on my affliction and my pain;
And forgive all my sins.
19 Behold my enemies, that they are many,
And hate me with cruel hatred.
20 Keep my soul, and rescue me;
Let me not be ashamed, for I have trusted in thee.
21 Let integrity and uprightness preserve me;
For I wait on thee.

22 Redeem Israel, O God,
Out of all his troubles!

PSALM XXVI.

[A Psalm] of David.

1 JUDGE me, O Jehovah;
For I have walked in my integrity,
And in Jehovah have I trusted;
I shall not waver.
2 Try me, O Jehovah, and test me;
Assay my reins and my heart.
3 For thy loving-kindness is before my eyes;
And I have walked in thy truth.
4 I have not sat with men of falsehood,
And I will not go in with dissemblers.
5 I have hated the congregation of evil-doers,
And I will not sit with the wicked.
6 I will wash my hands in innocency,
And will encompass thine altar, O Jehovah;
7 That I may publish, with the voice of thanksgiving,
And recount all thy wondrous works.
8 Jehovah, I have loved the habitation of thy house,
And the place where thy glory dwells.
9 Gather not my soul with sinners,
Nor my life with bloody men;
10 In whose hands is mischief,
And their right hand is full of bribes.
11 But as for me, I will walk in my integrity;
Redeem me, and be gracious to me.
12 My foot stands in an even place.
In the congregations will I bless Jehovah.

V. 2. Assay.] As a refiner of metals. The same word is used in Ps. 66 : 10, "thou hast assayed us, as silver is assayed."

V. 9. Gather.] Compare Gen. 25 : 8, and 49 : 33, "was gathered to his people."

PSALM XXVII.

[A Psalm] of David.

1 JEHOVAH is my light and my salvation ;
Of whom shall I be afraid ?
Jehovah is the stronghold of my life ;
Of whom shall I be in dread ?
2 When the wicked came upon me to eat up my flesh,
My foes and my enemies, it was they that stumbled and fell.
3 If a host shall encamp against me,
My heart will not fear ;
If war shall rise up against me,
In this will I be confident.
4 One thing have I asked of Jehovah,
That will I seek after ;
That I may dwell in the house of Jehovah all the days of my life,
To behold the beauty of Jehovah,
And to inquire in his temple.
5 For in the day of evil he will hide me in his pavilion ;
He will conceal me in the covert of his tabernacle ;
He will set me on high upon a rock.
6 And now shall my head be high above my enemies round about me ;
And I will offer in his tabernacle sacrifices of triumph ;
I will sing, and will praise Jehovah in song.
7 Hear, O Jehovah, my voice, I cry ;
And do thou be gracious to me, and answer me.
8 My heart has said to thee : SEEK YE MY FACE,—
Thy face, Jehovah, will I seek.
9 Hide not thy face from me ;
Turn not thy servant away in anger.
Thou hast been my help ;
Cast me not off, and forsake me not, O God of my salvation.

V. 8. The Psalmist repeats the divine command, SEEK YE MY FACE, in order to profess his obedience to it,—Thy face will I seek.

10 When my father and my mother have forsaken me,
Then Jehovah will receive me.
11 Teach me thy way, O Jehovah;
Lead me in a plain path, because of my enemies.
12 Give me not up to the will of my foes;
For false witnesses have risen up against me,
And such as breathe out violence.
13 Had I not believed that I should see the goodness of Jehovah,
In the land of the living!
14 Wait on Jehovah;
Be of good courage, and let thy heart be strong,
And wait on Jehovah.

PSALM XXVIII.

[A Psalm] of David.

1 UNTO thee, Jehovah, will I call.
My rock, be not deaf to me;
Lest thou be silent to me,
And I become like them that go down to the pit.
2 Hear the voice of my supplications when I cry to thee for help,
When I lift up my hands toward thy holy oracle.
3 Draw me not away with the wicked,
And with workers of iniquity;

V. 13. Had I not believed.] What would have followed such unbelief is more effectively implied by silence than expressed in words. The sentence is left incomplete by a common and very beautiful figure of speech (technically called *aposiopesis*), of which there are many examples in the Old and New Testaments. See Ex. 32 : 32, in the common English version: "Yet now, if thou wilt forgive their sin—; and if not, blot me, I pray thee, out of thy book which thou hast written."

For other examples, see Ps. 95 : 8; and in the New Testament, Acts 23 : 9, properly, If a spirit or an angel spoke to him—(revised version, according to the true text).

Who speak peace with their neighbors,
And mischief is in their heart.
4 Give them according to their doing,
And according to the evil of their deeds.
Give them according to the work of their hands;
Render to them their desert.
5 Because they regard not the works of Jehovah,
Nor the labor of his hands,
He will destroy them, and not build them up.
6 Blessed be Jehovah,
Because he has heard the voice of my supplications.
7 Jehovah is my strength and my shield;
In him my heart trusted, and I was helped,
And my heart shall triumph, and with my song will I
praise him.
8 Jehovah is strength to them;
And a stronghold of salvation is he to his anointed.
9 Save thy people,
And bless thy heritage,
And feed them, and bear them up forever!

PSALM XXIX.

A Psalm of David.

1 GIVE to Jehovah, ye sons of God,
Give to Jehovah glory and strength.
2 Give to Jehovah the glory of his name;
Worship Jehovah in the beauty of holiness.
3 The voice of Jehovah is on the waters;
The God of glory thunders;
Jehovah is on the great waters.
4 The voice of Jehovah is mighty;
The voice of Jehovah is full of majesty.

V. 1. Give.] Recognize as his; ascribe to him. Sons of God, as in Ps. 89 : 6, Job 1 : 6.

5 The voice of Jehovah breaks the cedars ;
And Jehovah breaks the cedars of Lebanon.
6 And he makes them skip like a calf,
Lebanon and Sirion like the young of the wild ox.
7 The voice of Jehovah cleaves out flames of fire.
8 The voice of Jehovah shakes the wilderness ;
Jehovah shakes the wilderness of Kadesh.
9 The voice of Jehovah makes the hinds bring forth,
And lays bare the forests ;
And in his palace, they all say, Glory !
10 Jehovah sat [in judgment] at the flood ;
And Jehovah sits a king forever.
11 Jehovah will give strength to his people ;
Jehovah will bless his people with peace.

PSALM XXX.

A Psalm,—a song for the Dedication of the House,—of David.

1 I WILL extol thee, Jehovah, for thou hast delivered me,
And hast not made my enemies rejoice over me.
2 Jehovah, my God,
I cried to thee for help, and thou didst heal me.

V. 6. Sirion.] The Sidonian name for Mount Hermon.

V. 7. Cleaves out flames of fire.] The forked lightning.

V. 9. His palace.] The universe ; the whole realm of nature, from which these illustrations of his power and majesty are drawn.

They all say.] In all his works there is a voice proclaiming, Glory ! The common English version, "in his temple doth every one speak of his glory," is a mistranslation, in which the sense and spirit of the original are lost.

Palace.] So the Hebrew word is properly translated, in Ps. 45 : 8, 15, 144 : 12 ; Prov. 30 : 28 ; Is. 13 : 22, 39 : 7, and elsewhere.

Ps. xxx. The occasion of the psalm is, most probably, referred to in 1 Chron. 22 : 1–5, the site of the future temple having then been dedicated as "the house of Jehovah God" (v. 1). The tone of sentiment is explained by the account given in the preceding chapter.

3 Jehovah, thou hast brought up my soul from the underworld;
Thou hast kept me alive, that I should not go down to the pit.
4 Sing praise to Jehovah, ye his saints,
And give praise to his holy memorial.
5 For his anger is for a moment; in his favor is life;
Weeping may endure for a night, but in the morning there is joy!
6 And as for me, in my prosperity I said,
I shall never be moved.
7 Jehovah, by thy favor thou madest my mountain stand strong;
Thou didst hide thy face,—I was troubled.
8 To thee, Jehovah, I call;
And to Jehovah I make supplication.
9 What profit is there in my blood,
When I go down to the pit?
Will dust praise thee? Will it declare thy truth?
10 Hear, O Jehovah, and be gracious to me;
Jehovah, be thou my helper!
11 Thou hast turned for me my mourning into dancing,
Thou hast loosed my sackcloth, and girded me with gladness;
12 In order that [my] glory may sing praise to thee, and not be silent.
Jehovah, my God, I will give thanks to thee forever.

V. 3. Thou hast brought up.] This is explained by the corresponding member, "thou hast kept me alive;" referring to the deliverance recorded in 2 Sam. ch. xxiv., and 1 Chron. ch. xxi.

V. 4. His holy memorial.] His sacred memorial name, JEHOVAH. See Ex. 3 : 15, "this is my name forever, and this is my memorial [memorial name] to all generations." Compare Hosea 12 : 5, "Jehovah is his memorial;" his memorial name, signifying what he is in his own nature, and bringing it to mind.

V. 12. My glory.] My nobler, spiritual nature. Compare the remark on Ps. 16 : 9.

PSALM XXXI.

To the chief Musician. A Psalm of David.

1 In thee, Jehovah, have I trusted,
Let me never be ashamed;
Deliver me in thy righteousness.
2 Incline to me thine ear, rescue me speedily.
Be thou to me for a rock of defense,
For a house of refuge, to save me.
3 For my rock and my fortress art thou;
And for thy name's sake thou wilt guide me and lead me.
4 Thou wilt bring me out from the net which they hid for me;
For thou art my defense.
5 Into thy hand I commit my spirit;
Thou hast redeemed me, Jehovah, God of truth!
6 I have hated them that regard lying vanities;
But I, in Jehovah do I trust.
7 I will exult and rejoice in thy kindness;
For thou hast seen my affliction,
Hast known the troubles of my soul;
8 And hast not shut me up in the hand of an enemy,
Hast set my feet in a large place.
9 Be gracious to me, Jehovah, for I am in trouble;
Wasted is my eye with grief, my soul, and my bowels.
10 For my life is spent with sorrow, and my years with sighing;
My strength fails because of my iniquity, and my bones are wasted.
11 Because of all my adversaries I am become a reproach,
And to my neighbors exceedingly, and a dread to my acquaintance.

Ps. xxxi. Of the same period, apparently, as Pss. vii. and xi.

V. 6. Vanities.] So idols are called in Deut. 32 : 21, as being "no gods" ("nothing in the world," 1 Cor. 8 : 4). They are here called lying vanities, in distinction from the "God of truth" (v. 5), as being false pretenders, deceiving those who trust in them.

When they saw me in the street they fled from me.
12 I am forgotten as a dead man out of mind;
I am become like a broken vessel.
13 For I heard the slander of many;
Terror was on every side, while they consulted together against me;
They plotted to take away my life.
14 But I, in thee did I trust, O Jehovah;
I said: Thou art my God.
15 My times are in thy hand;
Rescue me from the hand of my enemies and from my persecutors.
16 Cause thy face to shine upon thy servant;
In thy mercy save me.
17 Jehovah, let me not be ashamed, for I have called upon thee;
Let the wicked be ashamed, be put to silence in the underworld.
18 Let lying lips be struck dumb,
That speak rudely against the righteous,
In pride and scorn.
19 How great is thy goodness, which thou hast laid up for them that fear thee,
Hast wrought for them that trust in thee before the sons of men!
20 Thou wilt hide them in the covert of thy presence from the snares of man;
Thou wilt secrete them in a pavilion from the strife of tongues.
21 Blessed be Jehovah;
For he has shown me his marvelous kindness [as] in a strong city.
22 And yet I said, in my alarm,
I am cut off from before thine eyes.
But thou didst hear the voice of my supplications,
When I cried to thee for help.
23 Love Jehovah, all ye his saints.

Jehovah preserves the faithful,
And abundantly requites him that acts proudly.
24 Be of good courage, and let your heart be strong,
All ye that hope in Jehovah.

PSALM XXXII.

Didactic [Psalm] of David.

1 HAPPY he, whose transgression is forgiven, whose sin is
covered.
2 Happy the man,
To whom Jehovah imputes not iniquity,
And in whose spirit there is no guile.
3 When I kept silence, my bones wasted away,
Through my groaning all the day long.
4 For day and night thy hand was heavy upon me;
My moisture is turned into the droughts of summer. (*Pause.*)
5 I will make known to thee my sin, and my iniquity I have
not covered.
I said, I will confess my transgressions to Jehovah;
And thou forgavest the iniquity of my sin.
6 For this let every godly one pray to thee,
In a time when thou mayst be found.
Surely, in floods of great waters,
They will not come near him.
7 Thou art a hiding-place for me; thou wilt preserve me
from trouble;
Thou wilt surround me with songs of deliverance. (*Pause.*)
8 I will instruct thee, and will direct thee in the way that
thou shouldst go;
I will give counsel, with mine eye upon thee.

V. 8. With mine eye upon thee.] Not only guiding, but watching over thee.

9 Be not as the horse, as the mule, without understanding;
With bit and bridle his mouth is to be curbed,
Lest he come near to thee.
10 Many sorrows are to the wicked;
But he that trusts in Jehovah, mercy will encompass him.
11 Rejoice in Jehovah, and exult ye righteous;
And shout for joy, all ye upright in heart.

PSALM XXXIII.

1 Rejoice in Jehovah, ye righteous;
Praise is becoming to the upright.
2 Give praise to Jehovah with the harp;
With a ten-stringed lute sing praise to him.
3 Sing to him a new song;
Play skillfully with joyful sound.
4 For the word of Jehovah is right;
And all his work is in faithfulness.
5 He loves righteousness and judgment;
The earth is full of the kindness of Jehovah.
6 By the word of Jehovah were the heavens made,
And all their host by the breath of his mouth.
7 He gathered the sea as a heap;
He laid up the depths in storehouses.

V. 9. The objection to the common rendering of the second and third members, that this language is more appropriate to a wild beast than to the horse or mule, is not valid. The writer speaks of a heedless, unreasoning brute, whose motions, in order to be harmless to others, must be controlled by a superior intelligence.

V. 10, 2d member. *Or*, he will encompass him with mercy.

Ps. xxxiii. The position of the psalm in the first book, and its general tone and manner, indicate the royal Psalmist as the writer.

VV. 6, 7, are examples of numerous allusions to the earlier teachings of the book of Genesis, assumed to be familiar to the reader as the groundwork of all subsequent religious instruction. Such references should be carefully noted, as showing the relation of that book to subsequent revelations, and its place in the Divine Canon.

8 Let them be afraid of Jehovah, all the earth;
Let them stand in awe of him, all the inhabitants of the world,
9 For HE said it, and it was done;
HE commanded, and it stood fast.
10 Jehovah brought the counsels of the nations to naught;
He frustrated the devices of the peoples.
11 The counsel of Jehovah shall stand forever;
The devices of his heart to all generations.
12 Happy the nation, whose God is Jehovah,
The people he has chosen as a heritage for him!
13 Jehovah looks from heaven;
He sees all the sons of man;
14 From the place of his habitation he looks,
On all the inhabitants of the earth;
15 He that fashioned all their hearts,
That considers all their works.
16 The king is not saved by the multitude of a host;
A mighty man is not rescued by great strength.
17 The horse is a vain thing for safety,
And he will not deliver by his great strength.
18 Behold the eye of Jehovah is on them that fear him,
On them that hope in his mercy;
19 To rescue their soul from death,
And to keep them alive in famine.
20 Our soul has waited for Jehovah;
He is our help and our shield.
21 For in him shall our heart rejoice;
For we have trusted in his holy name.
22 Let thy mercy, Jehovah, be upon us,
According as we have hoped in thee.

V. 9. It will be observed, that the emphasis is not on the *act* ("said," common version "spake"), but on its subject, HE. The Psalmist calls on all men to fear JEHOVAH, and stand in awe of him; for HE it was who "said it, and it was done!"

V. 17. The horse.] The war-horse is meant, as is shown by the definite article. Compare Ps. 20 : 7.

PSALM XXXIV.

[A Psalm] of David, when he disguised his reason before Abimelech; and he drove him away, and he departed.

1 I WILL bless Jehovah at all times;
His praise shall ever be in my mouth.
2 My soul shall make her boast in Jehovah;
The humble will hear, and will be glad.
3 Magnify Jehovah with me,
And let us exalt his name together.
4 I sought Jehovah, and he answered me,
And from all my fears he delivered me.
5 They looked to him, and brightened;
And let not their faces blush.
6 This sufferer called, and Jehovah heard,
And saved him out of all his troubles.
7 The angel of Jehovah encamps around them that fear him,
And delivers them.
8 Taste and see that Jehovah is good;
Happy the man that trusts in him!
9 Fear Jehovah, ye his saints;
For there is no want to them that fear him.
10 Young lions lack, and suffer hunger;
But they that seek Jehovah shall want no good.
11 Come, ye sons, hearken to me;
I will teach you the fear of Jehovah.
12 Who is the man that desires life,
That loves days, that he may see good?

Ps. xxxiv. (title.) When he disguised.] This denotes the occasion of the psalm, written in after-life, and with reference to that occurrence. See 1 Sam. 21 : 13. Abimelech was the regal title of the king, whose personal name was Achish.

This is an *alphabetic* psalm, the letters of the Hebrew alphabet, in their regular order, being the initial letters of the successive couplets. This was doubtless intended to aid the memory; and it accounts for the peculiar composition of the psalm.

13 Keep thy tongue from evil,
And thy lips from speaking guile.
14 Depart from evil, and do good;
Seek peace, and pursue it.
15 The eyes of Jehovah are toward the righteous,
And his ears to their cry for help.
16 The face of Jehovah is against them that do evil,
To cut off their memory from the earth.
17 They cried, and Jehovah heard,
And rescued them out of all their troubles.
18 Jehovah is near to the broken in heart;
And he will save such as are contrite in spirit.
19 Many are the evils of the righteous;
But Jehovah will deliver him out of them all.
20 He keeps all his bones;
Not one of them is broken.
21 Evil will slay the wicked;
And they that hate the righteous shall be held guilty.
22 Jehovah redeems the soul of his servants,
And none shall be held guilty that trust in him.

PSALM XXXV.

[A Psalm] of David.

1 STRIVE, O Jehovah, with them that strive with me;
Fight against them that fight against me.
2 Lay hold of shield and buckler,
And stand up for my help.
3 And draw out the spear and shut up against my pursuers;
Say to my soul: I am thy salvation.
4 Let them be confounded and put to shame that seek for my soul;
Let them be turned back and put to confusion that devise my harm.

5 Let them be as chaff before the wind,
And the angel of Jehovah thrust them down.
6 Let their way be dark and slippery,
And the angel of Jehovah chase them.
7 For without cause they hid for me their pit-fall;
Without cause they digged it for my soul.
8 Let destruction come upon him unawares,
And his net which he hid, let it take him;
With destruction let him fall therein.
9 And my soul shall exult in Jehovah,
Shall rejoice in his salvation.
10 All my bones shall say:
Jehovah, who is like thee,
Rescuing the sufferer from one stronger than he,
The sufferer and the needy from his spoiler?
11 Cruel witnesses rise up against me;
What I am not conscious of they ask of me.
12 They requite me evil for good;
Forsaken is my soul!
13 But as for me, in their sickness my clothing was sackcloth;
I humbled my soul with fasting;
And my prayer will return into my bosom.
14 I behaved as if [it were] a friend, a brother to me;
I bowed down gloomily, as one that mourns for a mother.
15 But at my halting they rejoiced, and were gathered together;
The abject were gathered against me, and I knew it not;
They did tear, and ceased not.
16 Among hypocritical mockers for bread,
They gnashed upon me with their teeth.

V. 11. What I am not conscious of] Offenses of which I have no knowledge.

They ask of me.] Interrogating, with the malicious purpose of entrapping me. Compare the similar case in Luke 11 : 53, 54.

V. 15. Halting; from lameness, as one about to fall. Were gathered together; to triumph in his affliction.

V. 16. Mockers for bread.] Such as gain their bread, at the tables of the rich, by their talent for jesting and mimicry.

17 Lord, how long wilt thou look on?
Restore my soul from their destructions,
My life from the young lions.
18 I will give thee thanks in the great congregation;
In the multitude of people I will praise thee.
19 Let not them that are wrongfully my enemies rejoice over me,
Nor let them wink with the eye that hate me without cause.
20 For they speak not peace;
And against the quiet ones of the land,
They devise words of deceit.
21 And they open wide their mouth against me;
They have said: Aha! Aha!
Our eye has seen it.
22 Thou hast seen it, Jehovah; be not silent.
Lord, be not far from me.
23 Arouse thee, and awake for my right,
For my cause, my God, and my Lord.
24 Judge me according to thy righteousness, Jehovah, my God,
And let them not rejoice over me.
25 Let them not say in their heart: Aha! Our desire!
Let them not say: We have swallowed him up.
26 Let them be ashamed and put to confusion together,
That rejoice in my harm.
Let them be clothed with shame and dishonor,
They that act proudly against me.
27 Let those shout for joy and be glad that favor my just cause;
And let them ever say: Jehovah be magnified,
Who delights in the welfare of his servant.
28 And my tongue shall speak of thy righteousness,
Of thy praise all the day long.

VV. 17, 22, 23. Lord.] The word so rendered (not JEHOVAH, for which Lord is often substituted in the common version) has here the form denoting the Supreme Being.

V. 27. His servant.] The Psalmist speaks in this character. See the note on Ps. 18 : 50.

PSALM XXXVI.

To the chief Musician. [A Psalm] of the servant of Jehovah, of David.

1 THE transgression of the wicked says within my heart,
There is no fear of God before his eyes.
2 For he flatters himself in his own eyes,
Till his iniquity be found out, to be hated.
3 The words of his mouth are falsehood and deceit;
He has ceased to do wisely, to do well.
4 He devises mischief upon his bed;
He takes his stand upon a way that is not good;
He abhors not evil.
5 Jehovah, thy mercy is in the heavens,
And thy faithfulness unto the clouds.
6 Thy righteousness is like the mountains of God;
Thy judgments are a great deep;
Man and beast thou dost save, O Jehovah.
7 How precious is thy loving-kindness, O God;
And the sons of man may trust in the shadow of thy wings.
8 They shall be fully satisfied with the abundance of thy house;
And thou wilt make them drink of the river of thy pleasures.

V. 1. Says within my heart.] In my heart's interpretation of it. His transgression means, in the believer's just apprehension, that he has no fear of a God; a practical atheism.

Some Hebraists, following a different reading of the Hebrew text (his heart), translate: "The sinner has an oracle of wickedness within his heart;" meaning, the inspiration, or promptings, of a wicked heart. But everywhere else, the word rendered "wickedness" means transgression, or trespass, *in act*, not depravity or wickedness as an inward principle; and the strongest objection to the common rendering seems to be set aside by the above interpretation of it.

V. 2. Till his iniquity be found out.] Compare Gen. 44 : 16, "God has found out the iniquity of thy servants."

V. 6. Like the mountains of God.] Like his own mountains, vast and incomprehensible as these, the grandest of his works.

9 For with thee is the fountain of life;
In thy light shall we see light.
10 Continue thy loving-kindness to them that know thee,
And thy righteousness to the upright in heart.
11 Let not the foot of pride come against me,
And let not the hand of the wicked drive me away,
12 There are the workers of iniquity fallen;
They are thrust down, and will not be able to rise.

PSALM XXXVII.

[A Psalm] of David.

1 Fret not thyself at evil-doers;
Be not envious at workers of iniquity.
2 For they shall soon be cut down like the grass,
And wither as the green herb.
3 Trust in Jehovah and do good;
Dwell in the land, and feed securely.
4 And delight thyself in Jehovah;
And he will give thee the desires of thy heart.
5 Commit thy way to Jehovah;
And trust in him, and he will do it.
6 And he will bring out thy righteousness as the light,
And thy right as the noonday.
7 Be silent before Jehovah, and wait for him;
Fret not thyself at one that prospers in his way,
At the man who brings evil devices to pass.
8 Cease from anger, and forsake wrath;
Fret not thyself, [it is] only to do evil.

Ps. xxxvii. The psalm is written in *alphabetic* stanzas, nearly all of four lines each; the letters of the Hebrew alphabet, in regular order, being the initial letters of the successive stanzas. The psalm consists of disconnected aphorisms, which the alphabetic arrangement assisted in remembering.

V. 3, 2d member. *Or*, and feed on truth.

9 For evil-doers shall be cut off;
And those who wait on Jehovah, they shall inherit the land.
10 For yet a little while, and the wicked shall not be;
And thou shalt attentively consider his place, and it shall not be.
11 But the humble shall inherit the land,
And shall delight themselves in the abundance of peace.
12 The wicked plots against the righteous,
And gnashes upon him with his teeth.
13 The Lord will laugh at him;
For he sees that his day is coming.
14 The wicked have drawn out the sword,
And they have bent their bow,
To cast down the humble and needy,
To slay such as are of upright conduct.
15 Their sword shall enter into their own heart,
And their bows shall be broken.
16 Better is a little that the righteous man has,
Than the abundance of many wicked.
17 For the arms of the wicked shall be broken;
But Jehovah upholds the righteous.
18 Jehovah knows the days of the upright,
And their heritage shall be forever.
19 They shall not be ashamed in an evil time;
And in days of famine they shall be satisfied.
20 For the wicked shall perish;
And the enemies of Jehovah are as the beauty of the pastures;
They consume, in smoke they consume away.
21 The wicked borrows, and pays not;
But the righteous shows favor, and gives.
22 For they that are blessed of him shall inherit the land;
And they that are cursed of him shall be cut off.

V. 20. Beauty of the pastures.] The green grass, with which the pastures are clothed and adorned; a common image of short-lived prosperity and perishableness. Compare, for example, James 1 : 10, 11; Pss. 92 : 7, and 103 : 15.

23 A man's steps are ordered by Jehovah,
And he delights in his way.
24 For though he fall, he shall not be cast down;
For Jehovah upholds his hand.
25 I have been young, and have also become old;
And I have not seen the righteous forsaken,
Nor his seed begging bread.
26 All the day he shows favor, and lends;
And his seed are for a blessing.
27 Depart from evil, and do good,
And abide for evermore.
28 For Jehovah loves judgment,
And he will not forsake his saints.
They are preserved forever;
But the seed of the wicked is cut off.
29 The righteous shall inherit the land,
And shall dwell forever upon it.
30 The mouth of the righteous will utter wisdom,
And his tongue will speak what is right.
31 The law of God is in his heart;
His steps shall not waver.
32 The wicked watches for the righteous,
And seeks to slay him.
33 Jehovah will not leave him in his hand,
And will not condemn him when he is judged.

VV. 23, 24. A general proposition, commending a hopeful trust in Jehovah, on the ground that all a man's ways are ordered by him, and hence nothing really adverse can befall one who is in accord with him.

Delights in his way.] Takes delight in the course which he has himself marked out, and will therefore carry to completion.

The first member may be rendered:

By Jehovah are a man's steps established.

V. 26. For a blessing.] To themselves and others; enjoying and imparting good.

V. 27. Abide for evermore.] As in v. 29.

V. 28. Loves judgment.] The execution of justice, the maintenance of right.

V. 29. Dwell forever.] Not individually, but in their generations.

34 Wait on Jehovah, and keep his way,
And he will exalt thee, to inherit the land;
When the wicked are cut off, thou shalt see it.
35 I saw a wicked man in great power,
And spreading himself, like a tree flourishing in its native soil.
36 And one passed by, and behold, he was not;
And I sought him, and he could not be found.
37 Mark the perfect man, and behold the upright;
For there is a future to the man of peace.
38 But transgressors are destroyed together;
The future of the wicked is cut off.
39 And the salvation of the righteous is of Jehovah,
Their stronghold in time of trouble.
40 And Jehovah has helped them and delivered them.
He will deliver them from the wicked, and will save them,
For they have trusted in him.

PSALM XXXVIII.

A Psalm of David. To bring to remembrance.

1 JEHOVAH, do not in thy wrath rebuke me,
And do not in thy hot displeasure correct me.
2 For thine arrows are sunk into me,
And thy hand has come down upon me.
3 There is no soundness in my flesh, because of thine anger;
There is no health in my bones, because of my sin.
4 For my iniquities are gone over my head;
As a heavy burden, they are too heavy for me.
5 My stripes are putrid, and running,
Because of my foolishness.
6 I writhe, I am greatly bowed down;
I go mourning all the day long.

V. 37. There is a future.] Something that remains after him, in his posterity, in his children and his children's children. Compare vv. 27, 29. On the contrary, "transgressors are destroyed together," they and all that pertain to them.

7 For my loins are filled with burning;
And there is no soundness in my flesh.
8 I am benumbed and bruised exceedingly;
I cry out from the disquietude of my heart.
9 Lord, all my desire is before thee,
And my sighing is not hidden from thee.
10 My heart flutters, my strength fails me;
And the light of my eyes,—they also are gone from me.
11 My lovers and my friends stand aloof from my stroke,
And my neighbors stand afar off.
12 And they that seek for my soul lay snares,
And they that search for my harm speak mischievous things,
And they devise deceits all the day long.
13 But I, as a deaf man, hear not;
And as a dumb man opens not his mouth.
14 And I am as a man that hears not,
And in his mouth are no reproofs.
15 For for thee, Jehovah, do I wait;
Thou wilt answer, O Lord, my God.
16 For I said: Lest they shall rejoice over me,
Act proudly against me when my foot wavers.
17 For as for me, I am ready to halt,
And my sorrow is continually before me.
18 For I will declare my iniquity,
Will be anxious for my sin.
19 But my deadly enemies are strong,
And many are they that hate me without cause,
20 And that requite me evil for good;
They oppose me in return for my seeking good.
21 Forsake me not, O Jehovah;
My God, be not far from me.
22 Hasten to my help,
O Lord, my salvation.

V. 20. Seeking good.] Namely, their good, as the connection seems to require. Perhaps more generally, that which is right and good, the pursuit of which provokes their opposition.

PSALM XXXIX.

To the chief Musician, to Jeduthun. A Psalm of David.

1 I SAID: I will take heed to my ways,
That I sin not with my tongue.
I will keep a muzzle to my mouth,
While the wicked is before me.
2 I was dumb with silence;
I held my peace [even] from good,
And my sorrow was stirred.
3 My heart was hot within me.
While I muse, the fire kindles;
I spoke with my tongue:
4 Make me know, O Jehovah, my end,
And the measure of my days, what it is;
Let me know how frail I am!
5 Behold, thou hast made my days as handbreadths,
And my fleeting life is as nothing before thee.
Surely, a mere breath is every man in his best estate. (*Pause.*)
6 Surely, every man walks in a vain show;
Surely, they are disquieted in vain;
He heaps up treasures, and knows not who will gather them.
7 And now, Lord, what wait I for?
My hope, it is in thee.
8 Deliver me from all my transgressions;
Do not make me the reproach of fools.
9 I was dumb, I will not open my mouth,
Because thou didst it.

Ps. xxxix. (title.) Jeduthun was one of the three leaders of the temple music appointed by David (1 Chron. 25 : 1–7).

V. 2, 2d member. I refrained from utterance, altogether; even from that which is good, and might properly be spoken.

V. 6. A vain show.] A mere image, or likeness, unsubstantial and unreal.

V. 6, 2d member. *Or*, Surely, for a breath are they disquieted.

10 Remove thy stroke away from me;
I am consumed by the strife of thy hand.
11 With rebukes for iniquity thou dost correct man,
And waste as the moth what he delights in;
Surely, every man is vanity. (*Pause.*)
12 Hear my prayer, O Jehovah,
And give ear to my cry for help;
Hold not thy peace at my tears.
For I am a stranger with thee,
A sojourner, like all my fathers.
13 Look away from me, and let me cheer up,
Before I go hence, and be no more.

PSALM XL.

To the chief Musician. A Psalm of David.

1 I WAITED patiently for Jehovah,
And he inclined to me and heard my cry for help.
2 And he brought me up out of a horrible pit, out of the miry clay,
And set my feet upon a rock; he made my steps firm.
3 And he put in my mouth a new song,
Praise to our God.
Many will see, and fear,
And will trust in Jehovah.

V. 10. Strife of thy hand.] Conceived (as often elsewhere) as a controversy, on the part of God, with the subject of the infliction. Compare Hosea 4 : 1–3, 12 : 2.

V. 11. Rebukes for iniquity.] Not causeless and wanton strokes, but given for just cause, and for a desirable end.

V. 11. *Or*, Surely, every man is a breath.

V. 13. Look away from me.] Turn from me thy threatening look of displeasure.

V. 3. Fear.] A religious awe, inspired by true faith.

4 Happy the man,
Who has made Jehovah his trust,
And has not turned unto the proud and such as swerve to falsehood.
5 Many things hast thou done, Jehovah, my God;
Thy wonders, and thy thoughts toward us,
They can not be reckoned up in order unto thee.
I would declare and speak them,—
They are more than can be numbered.
6 Sacrifice and offering thou hast not desired;
My ears hast thou opened;
Burnt-offering and sin-offering thou hast not required.
7 Then said I: Lo, I come;
In the volume of the book it is written of me;
8 I delight to do thy will, O my God,
And thy law is within my heart.
9 I preached glad tidings of righteousness in the great congregation;
Lo, my lips I do not restrain,
Jehovah, thou knowest.
10 Thy righteousness I have not hid within my heart,
Thy faithfulness and thy salvation I have declared;
I have not concealed thy loving-kindness and thy truth from the great congregation.
11 Thou, O Jehovah,
Wilt not withhold thy compassions from me;
Thy loving-kindness and thy truth will ever preserve me.
12 For evils have gathered upon me, till they are without number;
My iniquities have overtaken me, and I can not behold them!

V. 4. Turned unto.] For counsel or help.—Swerved to falsehood.] From the ways of truth to falsehood and error.

V. 5, 3d member. *Or*, Nothing can be compared to thee.

V. 6. *Or*, My ears hast thou bored.

V. 12. I can not behold them.] Meaning, I can not bear the sight. In this sense the same words are used in Esther 8 : 6 (as rendered in the

They are more than the hairs of my head,
And my heart fails me.
13 Be pleased, O Jehovah, to rescue me;
Jehovah, hasten to my help.
14 Let them be ashamed and confounded together,
That seek after my soul to destroy it.
Let them be turned backward and put to shame,
That delight in my harm.
15 Let them be desolate because of their shame,
They that say to me, Aha! Aha!
16 Let all that seek thee rejoice and be glad in thee;
Let those say always, Jehovah be magnified,
Who love thy salvation.
17 But I am afflicted and needy, and the Lord will think upon me;
Thou art my help and my deliverer.
My God, do not delay!

PSALM XLI.

To the chief Musician. A Psalm of David.

1 HAPPY he that considers the poor!
In the day of evil Jehovah will deliver him.

---

common English version), "how *can I endure to see* the evil;" more literally, "how can I behold the evil."

Some understand the words to mean, "*I can not see* them all," they are more than can be seen; an unwarranted addition to the text, and without much point in the connection. Others translate, "my iniquities have overtaken me, and I am not able to see," through dimness of sight arising from great distress and consequent weakness; an unusual, and far from obvious, effect of conscious guilt. According to others, "I can not see" means, I can not see out, am so beset on every side that I have no outlook; another unusual effect of a consciousness of numerous sins.

These differences of opinion, and others that might be cited, show that the bearing of the expression, so simple in itself, is not without difficulty. The passage I have quoted from Esther 8 : 6 seems to me to suggest the true meaning; being the natural effect in one awakened to a consciousness of sins, which he can not bear to look upon.

2 Jehovah will keep him and preserve him alive ;
He shall be prospered in the land,
And thou wilt not give him up to the will of his enemies.
3 Jehovah will strengthen him on the couch of languishing ;
Thou wilt make all his bed in his sickness.
4 As for me, I said : Jehovah, be gracious to me ;
Heal my soul, for I have sinned against thee.
5 My enemies say evil of me :
When will he die, and his name perish?
6 And if he come to see, he speaks falsehood ;
In his heart he gathers up to himself mischief,
He goes forth, he tells it abroad.
7 Together they whisper against me, all they that hate me ;
Against me they devise my harm.
8 Some evil thing [they say] cleaves fast to him ;
And where he lies he shall rise up no more.
9 Yea, my familiar friend, in whom I trusted,
Who ate my bread, lifted the heel against me.
10 And thou, Jehovah, be gracious to me and raise me up,
That I may requite them.
11 By this I know that thou delightest in me,
Because my enemy shall not triumph over me.
12 And as for me, in my integrity thou hast upheld me,
And hast set me before thy face forever.

BLESSED BE JEHOVAH, GOD OF ISRAEL,
FROM EVERLASTING, AND TO EVERLASTING.
AMEN AND AMEN.

SECOND BOOK.

PSALMS XLII., XLIII.

To the Chief Musician. Didactic [Psalm] of the Sons of Korah.

1 As the hart pants after the water-brooks,
So does my soul pant for thee, O God.
2 My soul thirsts for God, for the living God;
When shall I come, and appear before God!
3 My tears have become my food day and night,
While they continually say to me, Where is thy God?
4 These things will I call to mind,
And pour out my heart within me,
When I shall pass along in the thick crowd,
Shall move onward with them to the house of God,
With the voice of joy and praise, a festive throng.
5 Why art thou bowed down, my soul,
And art disquieted within me?
Hope thou in God; for I shall yet praise him,
The help of my countenance, and my God.

Pss. xlii. and xliii. are properly one Psalm, as in many Hebrew manuscripts. The Psalm is in the strophic form (Introduction, § 8, 4), divided into three nearly equal parts by the refrain in Ps. 42 : 5, 11, Ps. 43 : 5. For the occasion of the Psalm, see the remarks on Ps. iii.

Title: Of the Sons of Korah.] See the Introduction, § 4, third paragraph.

V. 3. They] Whether adversaries, or desponding friends, as in Ps. 3 : 2.

6 My soul is bowed down within me;
Therefore will I remember thee from the land of Jordan,
And of the Hermons, from the mount Mizar.
7 Deep calls to deep, at the noise of thy water-falls;
All thy waves and thy billows are gone over me.
8 By day will Jehovah command his loving-kindness,
And by night shall his song be with me,
A prayer to the God of my life.
9 I will say to God my rock: Why hast thou forgotten me?
Why do I go mourning for the oppression of the enemy?
10 As with a crushing in my bones my enemies reproach me,
While they continually say to me: Where is thy God?
11 Why art thou bowed down, my soul,
And why art thou disquieted within me?
Hope thou in God; for I shall yet praise him,
The help of my countenance, and my God.
1 Judge me, O God, and plead my cause;
From an ungodly nation,
From the deceitful and unjust man, thou wilt deliver me.
2 For thou art the God of my strength;
Why hast thou cast me off?
Why do I go mourning for the oppression of the enemy?
3 Send out thy light and thy truth;
They shall guide me;
They shall bring me to thy holy mount,
And to thy tabernacles.
4 And I shall come to the altar of God,
To God, my exceeding joy;
And I will praise thee upon the harp, O God, my God.
5 Why art thou bowed down, my soul,
And why art thou disquieted within me?
Hope thou in God; for I shall yet praise him,
The help of my countenance and my God.

V. 6. The Hermons.] The three summits of Mt. Hermon

PSALM XLIV.

To the Chief Musician. Didactic [Psalm] of the Sons of Korah.

1 O God, we have heard with our ears,
Our fathers have told us,
The work thou didst work in their days,
In the days of old.
2 Thou with thy hand didst dispossess the heathen, and them thou plantedst;
Didst crush peoples, and them thou didst extend.
3 For not by their sword did they possess the land,
And their arm did not save them;
But thy right hand, and thy arm, and the light of thy countenance,
Because thou didst favor them.
4 Thou art he, my king, O God;
Command deliverances for Jacob.
5 Through thee shall we push down our foes;
Through thy name shall we tread them under that rise up against us.
6 For I will not trust in my bow;
And my sword will not save me.
7 For thou hast saved us from our foes,
And them that hate us thou hast put to shame.
8 In God will we glory all the day,
And thy name forever will we praise. (*Pause.*)
9 Yet thou didst cast us off, and put us to shame;
And thou goest not forth with our armies.
10 Thou makest us turn back from the foe,
And they that hate us spoil for themselves.
11 Thou givest us as sheep for food,
And scatterest us among the heathen.
12 Thou sellest thy people for naught,
And hast not increased by their price.
13 Thou makest us a reproach to our neighbors,
A scorn and a derision to them that are about us.

14 Thou makest us a by-word among the heathen,
A shaking of the head among the peoples.
15 All the day my disgrace is before me,
And the shame of my face covers me;
16 For the voice of him that reproaches and blasphemes,
On account of the enemy and revenger.
17 All this is come upon us; and we have not forgotten thee,
And have not been false to thy covenant.
18 Our heart has not turned back,
Nor our steps declined from thy way;
19 That thou shouldst have crushed us in the place of howling beasts,
And covered over us with the shadow of death.
20 If we have forgotten the name of our God,
And spread out our hands to a strange god;
21 Shall not God search this out?
For he knows the secrets of the heart.
22 Because for thy sake we are slain all the day long,
Are accounted as sheep for slaughter.
23 Arouse thee; why sleepest thou, O Lord?
Awake; do not cast off forever.
24 Wherefore hidest thou thy face,
Forgettest our affliction and our oppression?
25 For our soul is bowed down to the dust,
Our belly cleaves to the earth.
26 Arise, a help for us,
And redeem us for thy mercy's sake.

PSALM XLV.

To the Chief Musician. After [the melody] "Lilies." Didactic [Psalm] of the Sons of Korah. A Song of Delights.

1 My heart is overflowing with a goodly theme.
I say: My work is for a king;

V. 1. *Or*, My works are for a king. *Or*, I utter my work [*i. e*, poem] for a king.

My tongue is the pen of a ready writer.
2 Fair, fair art thou, above the sons of men;
Grace is poured into thy lips;
Therefore has God blessed thee forever.
3 Gird thy sword on the thigh, O Mighty One,
Thy honor and thy majesty;
4 And in thy majesty ride prosperously,
For the sake of truth and humble right,
And thy right hand will teach thee fearful deeds.
5 Thine arrows are sharp,
In the hearts of the king's enemies;
Peoples shall fall under thee.
6 Thy throne, O God, is forever and ever;
A sceptre of righteousness is the sceptre of thy kingdom.
7 Thou hast loved righteousness, and hated wickedness;
Therefore, God, thy God, has anointed thee,
With the oil of gladness above thy fellows.
8 Myrrh and aloes, cassia, are all thy garments;
From palaces of ivory stringed instruments cheer thee.
9 Daughters of kings are among thy precious ones;
At thy right hand stands the queen, in gold of Ophir.
10 Hearken, daughter, and behold, and incline thine ear;
And forget thy people and thy father's house;
11 And let the king desire thy beauty;
For he is thy lord, and do thou do him homage.
12 And the daughter of Tyre with a gift shall court thy favor,
The rich ones of the people.
13 All glorious is the king's daughter within;
Of gold embroidery is her apparel.

V. 5. The order of the members, as they now stand in the Hebrew text, is as follows:

Thine arrows are sharp,—
Peoples shall fall under thee,—
In the heart of the king's enemies.

V. 12. Daughter of Tyre, for the city and its inhabitants, personified as a female. Compare Is. 37 : 22.

14 In gayly wrought garments she shall be conducted to the king,
Virgins behind her, her companions,
Brought in to thee.
15 They shall be conducted with gladness and rejoicing;
They shall enter in to the palace of the king.
16 In place of thy fathers shall be thy sons;
Thou shalt set them for princes in all the earth.
17 I will cause thy name to be remembered in all generations;
Therefore shall peoples praise thee forever and ever.

PSALM XLVI.

To the Chief Musician. To [voices of] Maidens. A Song of the Sons of Korah.

1 God is to us a refuge and strength;
A help in troubles, most surely found.
2 Therefore we will not fear, though the earth change,
Though the mountains be moved into the heart of the seas.
3 Let its waters roar and foam,
Let the mountains shake with the swelling thereof. (*Pause.*)
4 There is a river, whose streams gladden the city of God,
The holy place of the dwellings of the Most High.
5 God is in the midst of her; she shall not be moved;
God will help her, at the turning of the morning.
6 The heathen raged, kingdoms were moved;
He uttered his voice, the earth melted.
7 Jehovah of hosts is with us;
The God of Jacob is a refuge for us. (*Pause.*)

V. 1. Surely found.] Compare Deut. 4 : 29; 1 Chr. 28 : 9; 2 Chr. 15 : 2, 4, 15; Is. 55 : 6; 65 : 1; Jer. 29 : 14.

V. 5. At the turning of the morning.] At the crisis, when darkness begins to give place to light, and morning is about to dawn.

8 Come, see the deeds of Jehovah,
Who has made desolations in the earth;
9 Causing wars to cease to the end of the earth;
The bow he breaks, and cuts the spear asunder,
The chariots he burns in the fire.
10 Desist, and know that I am God;
I will be exalted among the heathen, I will be exalted in the earth.
11 Jehovah of hosts is with us;
The God of Jacob is a refuge for us.

PSALM XLVII.

To the Chief Musician. A Psalm of the Sons of Korah.

1 All ye peoples, clap your hands;
Shout unto God with the voice of triumph.
2 For Jehovah, Most High, is terrible;
A great king over all the earth.
3 He will subdue peoples under us,
And nations under our feet.
4 He will choose for us our inheritance,
The pride of Jacob, whom he loved. (*Pause.*)
5 God has gone up with shouting,
Jehovah with sound of trumpet.
6 Sing praise to God, sing praise;
Sing praise to our king, sing praise.
7 For God is king of all the earth;
Sing praise, in instructive song.
8 God reigns over the heathen;
God sits on his holy throne.
9 Nobles of the peoples are assembled,
The people of the God of Abraham.
For to God belong the shields of the earth;
He is greatly exalted.

V. 9. Peoples.] A frequent designation of the tribes of Israel, together constituting "the people of the God of Abraham."

PSALM XLVIII.

A Song. A Psalm of the Sons of Korah.

1 Great is Jehovah, and greatly to be praised,
In the city of our God, his holy mount.
2 Beautiful in elevation, the joy of the whole earth,
Mount Zion, the sides of the north,
The city of the great King!
3 God is known in her palaces for a refuge.
4 For lo, the kings were assembled,
They passed along together.
5 They saw; then they marveled;
They were dismayed, they fled away.
6 Trembling took hold on them there,
Pain, as of a woman in travail.
7 With an east wind,
Thou breakest the ships of Tarshish.
8 As we have heard, so have we seen,
In the city of Jehovah of hosts, in the city of our God;
God will establish it forever. (*Pause.*)
9 We have thought of thy loving-kindness, O God,
In the midst of thy temple.
10 As is thy name, O God,
So is thy praise, unto the ends of the earth;
Thy right hand is full of righteousness.
11 Let Mount Zion rejoice,
Let the daughters of Judah exult,
Because of thy judgments.
12 Walk about Zion, and go round about her;
Number her towers.
13 Mark well her rampart,
Go through her palaces,
That ye may tell it to the generation following.
14 For this God is our God forever and ever;
He will guide us, until death.

PSALM XLIX.

To the Chief Musician. A Psalm of the Sons of Korah.

1 Hear this, all ye peoples,
Give ear, all ye inhabitants of the world;
2 Both men of low and men of high degree,
Rich and poor together.
3 My mouth shall speak wisdom,
And the meditation of my heart is understanding.
4 I will incline my ear to a parable;
I will open my dark saying on the harp.
5 Wherefore should I fear in days of evil,
When the iniquity of my supplanters compasses me about;
6 Who trust in their might,
And glory in the abundance of their wealth?
7 A brother can no one by any means redeem,
Or give to God a ransom for him;
8 (For costly is the redemption of their soul,
And it forever fails;)
9 That he should live on forever,
Should not see the pit.
10 For he shall see it. Wise men die,
Alike, the fool and the brutish perish;
And they leave their wealth to others.
11 Their inward thought is, that their houses are forever,
Their dwellings to all generations;
They call their lands after their own names.
12 But man, in honor, continues not;
He is like the beasts that perish.

V. 5. Supplanters.] Compare the use of the Hebrew word in Gen. 27 : 36, "he has supplanted me;" properly, to take one by the heel in order to throw him down, and hence to deal treacherously with him.

V. 7. Redeem.] From temporal death, which is meant by "redemption of their soul," in v. 8.

13 This is their way, to whom folly belongs;
And they that come after them will delight in their sayings. (*Pause.*)
14 Like sheep they are laid in the grave;
Death shall feed on them;
And the upright shall rule over them in the morning;
And their form shall consume in the grave from its dwelling.
15 But God will redeem my soul from the power of the grave;
For he will take me.
16 Do not fear, because one becomes rich,
Because the glory of his house increases.
17 For, when he dies, he shall take nothing away;
His glory shall not descend after him.
18 Though in his life he bless his soul,
And men praise thee that thou doest well for thyself,
19 It shall come to the generation of his fathers;
They shall never see light.
20 Man that is in honor, and understands not,
Is like the beasts that perish.

PSALM L.

A Psalm of Asaph.

1 THE Mighty One, God, Jehovah, has spoken,
And has called the earth,
From the rising of the sun unto its going down.

VV. 14, 15. Contrast between the end of the wicked and the righteous. The former are laid in the grave like brutes, with no hope of a joyful morning after the night of death, when the upright, oppressed in this life, shall triumph over them. The latter shall be redeemed from the power of the grave; he shall not remain under it forever. It is absurd to suppose, as some interpret the writer's language, that he looked for exemption from temporal death, declared in v. 10 to be the lot common to all.

From its dwelling.] From its abode in the material substance which bore their organized shape and form.

V. 18. Bless his soul.] Count himself happy.

2 Out of Zion, the perfection of beauty,
God has shined forth.
3 Our God will come, and shall not keep silence;
A fire will devour before him,
And round him tempests rage with violence.
4 He will call to the heavens above,
And to the earth, that he may judge his people;
5 Gather to me my saints,
Who have made a covenant with me by sacrifice.
6 And the heavens declare his righteousness;
For God, he is judge. (*Pause.*)
7 Hear, O my people, and I will speak,
O Israel, and I will testify against thee;
I am God, thy God.
8 Not for thy sacrifices will I reprove thee;
And thy burnt-offerings are continually before me.
9 I will not take a bullock from thy house,
Nor he-goats from thy folds.
10 For mine is every beast of the forest,
The cattle on a thousand hills.
11 I know every bird of the mountains,
And the beasts of the field are before me.
12 If I were hungry, I would not say it to thee;
For the world is mine, and the fullness thereof.
13 Will I eat the flesh of bulls,
And drink the blood of goats?
14 Sacrifice to God thanksgiving,
And pay to the Most High thy vows.
15 And call upon me in the day of trouble;
I will deliver thee, and thou shalt honor me.
16 And to the wicked God says:
What right hast thou to declare my statutes,
And take my covenant into thy mouth;
17 While thou dost hate instruction,
And cast my words behind thee?
18 If thou seest a thief, thou delightest in him,
And with adulterers is thy portion.

19 Thy mouth thou hast given up to evil,
And thy tongue contrives deceit.
20 Thou sittest, and speakest against thy brother;
At thy mother's son thou dost give a thrust.
21 These things hast thou done, and I kept silence.
Thou thoughtest I was surely such as thyself.
I will reprove thee, and will array them before thine eyes.
22 O consider this, ye that forget God,
Lest I tear in pieces, and there be no deliverer.
23 He that sacrifices thanksgiving shall honor me;
And he that directs his way,
To him will I show the salvation of God.

PSALM LI.

To the Chief Musician. A Psalm of David; when Nathan the prophet came to him, after he went in to Bathsheba.

1 Be gracious to me, O God, according to thy loving-kindness;
According to the greatness of thy compassion blot out my transgressions.
2 Wash me thoroughly from my iniquity,
And from my sin make me clean.
3 For my transgressions I know,
And my sin is before me continually.
4 Toward thee, thee only, have I sinned,
And done the evil in thy sight;
That thou mayest be just when thou speakest,
Be pure when thou judgest.
5 Behold, in iniquity was I brought forth,
And in sin did my mother conceive me.
6 Behold, thou desirest truth in the reins,
And in the hidden part thou wilt make me know wisdom.

V. 23. He that sacrifices thanksgiving.] Compare v. 14.

7 Thou wilt purge me of sin with hyssop, and I shall be clean;
Thou wilt wash me, and I shall be whiter than snow.
8 Thou wilt make me hear joy and gladness;
The bones thou hast broken shall exult.
9 Hide thy face from my sins,
And blot out all my iniquities.
10 Create in me a clean heart, O God,
And renew a right spirit within me.
11 Cast me not away from thy presence,
And take not thy holy Spirit from me.
12 Restore to me the joy of thy salvation,
And with a free spirit uphold me.
13 I will teach transgressors thy ways,
And sinners shall return to thee.
14 Deliver me from blood-guiltiness, O God,
O God of my salvation;
My tongue shall sing aloud of thy righteousness.
15 O Lord, thou wilt open my lips,
And my mouth shall declare thy praise.
16 For thou desirest not sacrifice, else would I give it;
In burnt-offering thou delightest not.
17 The sacrifices of God are a broken spirit;
A broken and contrite heart, O God, thou wilt not despise.
18 Do good, in thy good pleasure, to Zion;
Thou wilt build the walls of Jerusalem.
19 Then wilt thou be pleased with sacrifices of righteousness, with burnt-offering, and whole burnt-offering;
Then shall they offer bullocks upon thine altar.

PSALM LII.

To the chief Musician. Didactic [Psalm] of David, when Doeg the Edomite came and told Saul, and said: David came to the house of Ahimelech.

1 WHY dost thou boast in evil, O mighty man?
The goodness of God is continual.

V. 12. Free spirit.] Freely bestowed. Ps. lii. (title.) See 1 Sam. 22 : 9.

2 Thy tongue devises mischiefs,
Like a sharpened razor, working deceit.
3 Thou lovest evil more than good;
Lying, more than to speak righteousness. (*Pause.*)
4 Thou lovest all devouring words,
O deceitful tongue.
5 God will also destroy thee forever.
He will lay hold of thee, and pluck thee out of the tent,
And uproot thee from the land of the living. (*Pause.*)
6 And the righteous will see, and fear,
And will laugh at him:
7 Behold the man,
That makes not God his strength,
And trusts in the abundance of his riches,
Is strong in his wickedness.
8 But I am like a green olive-tree in the house of God;
I trust in the mercy of God forever and ever.
9 I will praise thee forever, because thou didst it;
And will wait on thy name, for it is good before thy saints.

PSALM LIII.

To the chief Musician. Of [moral] disease. Didactic [Psalm] of David.

1 The fool has said in his heart: There is no God.
Corrupt and abominable are they in iniquity;
There is none that doeth good.
2 God looked down from heaven upon the sons of men,
To see if there is any that understands,
That seeks after God.
3 They have all turned back; one and all are they polluted;
There is none that doeth good, not even one.
4 Have the workers of iniquity no knowledge,
Who eat up my people as they eat bread,
Call not upon God?

Ps. liii. A Psalm of David (Ps. xiv) adapted, by slight changes, to some later national occurrence.

5 There were they in great fear, where no fear was;
For God has scattered the bones of thy besiegers.
Thou hast put them to shame, because God despised them.
6 Oh for the salvation of Israel out of Zion!
When God turns the captivity of his people,
Jacob will exult, Israel will rejoice.

PSALM LIV.

To the chief Musician. With stringed instruments. Didactic [Psalm] of David, when the Ziphites came, and said to Saul: Is not David hiding himself with us?

1 O God, by thy name save me,
And in thy might judge me.
2 O God, hear my prayer;
Give ear to the words of my mouth.
3 For strangers have risen up against me,
And the violent seek after my soul;
They have not set God before them. (*Pause.*)
4 Behold, God is a helper for me;
The Lord is with them that uphold my soul.

V. 5. There.] Pointing to some recent and familiar occurrence. No fear.] Either no occasion of fear, or no apprehension of coming evil. Of the former case an illustration may be found in 2 Kings ch. vii. (compare vv. 6, 7, and 14, 15); of the latter, in Is. xxxvii. 36.

V. 6. Turns the captivity.] Compare the note on Job 42 : 10. Israel is another name for Jacob, with the accessory idea of "prevailing with God;" see Gen. 32 : 28. Jacob, on the contrary, is expressive of weakness; see, for example, Amos 7 : 2. By both are meant God's people; one implying their weakness in themselves, the other, their strength in God.

Ps. liv. (title.) When the Ziphites came.] For the historical allusion see 1 Sam. 23 : 19.

V. 1. Thy name; as representing God, and in him all in which the believer trusts, and finds security.

V. 3. Stranger.] A foreigner, not an Israelite; but also one estranged in spirit, an enemy, thus including those named in the title.

V. 4. *Or*, The Lord is he that upholds my soul.

5 He will return the evil to my enemies;
In thy truth cut them off.
6 With a free-will-offering will I sacrifice to thee;
I will praise thy name, Jehovah, for it is good.
7 For out of all distress has he delivered me,
And my eye has seen its desire on my enemies.

PSALM LV.

To the chief Musician. With stringed instruments. Didactic [Psalm] of David.

1 Give ear, O God, to my prayer,
And do not hide thyself from my supplication.
2 Attend to me, and answer me.
I am restless in my complaining, and disquieted;
3 Because of the voice of the enemy, on account of the oppression of the wicked.
For they cause mischief to impend over me,
And in anger lay a snare for me.
4 My heart quakes within me.
And terrors of death have fallen upon me.
5 Fear and trembling enter into me,
And horror overwhelms me.
6 And I say: Oh that I had wings like the dove;
I would fly away, and be at rest!

V. 5. *Or*, The evil will return to my enemies.

V. 5, 2d member. In thy truth.] As faithfulness to his word requires.

V. 7. Has seen its desire.] The Hebrew verb, in its construction here, means to gaze intently, and also to look upon with satisfaction, as in this case on a vanquished enemy. See the remark on Ps. 18 : 50, and compare the article "Psalms, Imprecatory," in *Smith's Bible Dictionary* (American edition, p. 2625), particularly divisions iv. and v.

V. 3. Impend over me.] The image is of a wall, or a tower, tottering and ready to fall and crush the victim. So do they keep me in continual apprehension of coming evil.

7 Lo, I would wander far away,
I would lodge in the wilderness. (*Pause.*)
8 I would make haste to escape,
From the stormy wind, from the tempest.
9 Destroy, O Lord; divide their tongue;
For I have seen violence and strife in the city.
10 Day and night they go about her on her walls,
And trouble and sorrow are within her.
11 Corruption is within her,
And from her market-place depart not extortion and deceit.
12 For it is not an enemy that reproaches me, else I could bear it;
Not one that hates me has acted proudly against me,
Else I would hide myself from him;
13 But thou—a man esteemed my equal,
My associate and my familiar friend.
14 Together we hold sweet familiar converse,
Walk to the house of God in the festal crowd.
15 Desolations are upon them; they shall go down alive to the underworld;
For wickedness is in their dwelling, in the midst of them.
16 As for me, I will call upon God,
And Jehovah will save me.
17 Evening, and morning, and noon, will I lament and sigh,
And he will hear my voice.

V. 9. Divide their tongue.] The tongue being the instrument of communication, the meaning is, make division in their counsels; set them at variance, and thus thwart their purposes.

V. 11. Market place.] A broad open space at the gate of a city, where the people assembled for the transaction of business, and where magistrates sat to administer justice. Compare Neh. 8 : 1 (properly, "into the broad space that was before the water-gate"), 2 Chron. 32 : 6 (properly, "in the broad space at the gate of the city"), Job 5 : 4 (with the references in the writer's note) and 29 : 7.

V. 15. Go down alive.] As they who opposed the authority of God in the person of his servant Moses (Numb. ch. xvi.).

V. 15 2d member. In the midst of them.] *Or*, within them (in their heart)

18 He redeemed my soul in peace from the war against me;
For many were [engaged] with me.
19 God will hear, and he will answer them,—
Even he that sits [as judge] of old,— (*Pause.*)
To whom there were no changes,
And they feared not God.
20 He put forth his hand against those at peace with him;
He profaned his covenant.
21 Smooth are the buttered tones of his mouth,
But his heart is war.
Softer than oil are his words,
But they are drawn swords.
22 Cast thy burden on Jehovah,
And he will sustain thee.
He will never suffer the righteous man to be moved.
23 But thou, O God, wilt bring them down to the pit of destruction.
Bloody and deceitful men shall not live half their days.
But as for me, I will trust in thee.

PSALM LVI.

To the chief Musician. After [the melody] "The mute dove in far-off lands." Memorial [Psalm] of David, when the Philistines seized him in Gath.

1 Be gracious to me, O God, for man would devour me.
Continually fighting he oppresses me.
2 Daily would my enemies devour me;
For many are they that fight against me proudly.

V. 19. Will answer them.] In the just reward of their misdeeds.

V. 19, 3d member. No changes.] No vicissitudes of fortune.

V. 20. He put forth.] Individualizing the many opposers (vv. 18, 19), or referring especially to the subject of vv. 12–14.

V. 20. Profaned his covenant.] Violated its sanctity, by a breach of its obligations. Compare Malach. 2 : 10.

3 What time I am afraid,
I will put my trust in thee.
4 In God will I praise his word;
In God do I trust, I will not fear;
What can flesh do to me?
5 Every day they wrest my words;
Against me are all their thoughts for evil.
6 They gather together, they lie in wait;
They, my supplanters, watch,
As they have waited for my soul.
7 Shall they escape by iniquity?
In anger bring down the peoples, O God.
8 My wanderings hast thou numbered.
Put thou my tears in thy bottle;
Are they not in thy reckoning?
9 Then shall my enemies turn back when I cry;
This I know, for God is for me.
10 In God will I praise the word;
In Jehovah will I praise the word.
11 In God do I trust, I will not fear;
What can man do to me?
12 On me, O God, are thy vows;
I will pay thanksgivings unto thee.
13 For thou hast delivered my soul from death.
Wilt thou not [deliver] my feet from stumbling,
That I may walk before God,
In the light of life?

V. 4, 1st member. In God.] The ground of praise being in him, as is also the ground of trust (next line).

V. 6, 2d member. *Or,* They who watch my heels (to trip me).

V. 8. Numbered.] As in Job 31:4, Does he not see my ways, and number all my steps? That is, does he not take account of all, so that none escape observation?

V. 9, 2d member. *Or,* This I know, that God is for me.

V. 10. The word.] The word of promise, that God is for me, as expressed in the preceding sentence. In God—in Jehovah.] As in v. 4.

V. 13, 4th member. Light of life.] In contrast with the darkness and gloom of the realm of death. Compare Job 10 : 21, 22

PSALM LVII.

To the chief Musician. Do not Destroy. Memorial [Psalm] of David, when he fled from Saul, in the cave.

1 Be gracious to me, O God, be gracious to me,
For in thee has my soul sought refuge ;
And in the shadow of thy wings will I seek refuge,
Until the calamities shall pass by.
2 I will cry unto God Most High,
To the Mighty, who completes [the purpose] concerning me.
3 He will send from heaven and save me,
Whom he that would devour me has reviled ; (*Pause.*)
God will send his mercy and his truth.
4 My soul is in the midst of lions ;
I will lie down with them that breathe out flames,
Sons of men whose teeth are spears and arrows,
And their tongue a sharp sword.
5 Be thou exalted above the heavens, O God,
Thy glory over all the earth !
6 They prepared a net for my steps ;
He bowed down my soul.
They dug a pit before me ;
They fell into the midst of it. (*Pause.*)
7 My heart is fixed, O God, my heart is fixed ;
I will sing, and will sing praise.

Ps. lvii. (title). Do not destroy.] A designation (perhaps suggested by Deut. 9 : 26) of a group of psalms by David (Pss. lvii–lix.) and of Ps. lxxv. As a motto, it is appropriate to the subject, or the occasion, of them all.—When he fled.] See 1 Sam., ch. xxii. (or ch. xxiv.).

V. 2. Completes—concerning me.] Does not leave unfinished what he has purposed and begun. This specific idea, of a purpose to be fulfilled, is lost in the vague rendering, "performeth all things for me."

V. 3, 3d member. Mercy and Truth personified. His mercy, in compassion for me ; his truth, in fidelity to his promises.

V. 4, 2d member. I will lie down.] The language of cheerful confidence in God's protecting care. *Or*, With them that lick [the jaws]. See the preceding member.

V. 6, 2d member. He.] The author and animating spirit of these persecutions, his royal adversary.

8 Awake my glory, awake lute and harp;
I will awake the dawn!
9 I will praise thee among the peoples, O Lord;
I will sing praise to thee among the nations.
10 For great, unto the heavens, is thy mercy,
And unto the clouds thy truth.
11 Be thou exalted above the heavens, O God,
Thy glory over all the earth!

PSALM LVIII.

To the chief Musician. Do not Destroy. Memorial [Psalm] of David.

1 Do ye, in truth, with silence speak righteousness?
With equity do ye judge, ye sons of men?
2 Yea, in heart ye work iniquities,
And mete out the violence of your hands in the land.
3 The wicked are estranged from the womb;
From birth they go astray, speaking lies.
4 They have poison like the poison of a serpent;
As a deaf adder stops its ear,
5 That hearkens not to the voice of enchanters,
Of one charming with charms, well-skilled.
6 O God, break their teeth in their mouth;
The fangs of the young lions beat out, O Jehovah.
7 They shall melt away, as waters flow off;
He will fit his arrows, they shall be as if severed.
8 As a snail melts as it goes,
An untimely birth of a woman,—they have not seen the sun.

Ps. lviii. (title). Do not destroy.] As in Ps. lvii. (title).

V. 1. With silence, etc.] A bitter sarcasm. Is it with silence that ye perform the office of speech? Dumb, when ye ought to speak, and declare the right!

V. 2. In heart.] The heart itself being a fountain only of evil.

V. 4. *Or*, As a deaf adder, he stops his ear.

V. 8. They are like the snail, that dissolves in slime as it goes; like the untimely birth, that has never seen the sun. So do they melt away; so short their life, it is as though they had not lived at all.

9 Before your pots can feel the thorns,
As well green as burning, he will sweep it away with a tempest.
10 The righteous will rejoice that he has seen vengeance;
His steps he will bathe in the blood of the wicked.
11 And men will say: Verily, there is fruit for the righteous;
Verily, there is a God that judges in the earth.

PSALM LIX.

To the chief Musician. Do not Destroy. Memorial [Psalm] of David, when Saul sent, and they watched the house to slay him.

1 DELIVER me from my enemies, O my God;
Thou wilt set me on high from them that rise up against me.
2 Deliver me from workers of iniquity,
And from men of blood save me.
3 For lo, they lie in wait for my soul;
Strong ones are gathered against me,
Not for my transgression, and not for my sin, O Jehovah.
4 For no iniquity, they run and prepare themselves;
Awake, to meet me, and behold.
5 And thou Jehovah, God of hosts,
God of Israel,
Awake to visit all the heathen;
Spare no iniquitous traitors. (*Pause.*)

V. 9. Before, etc.] Before your schemes can be matured and carried into effect.—Thorns.] Used as fuel; compare Eccl. 7 : 6.

V. 9, 2d member. As well green as burning.] In every stage of progress, as well incipient as final.—Sweep it away.] Comprehending all in one.

Ps. lix. (title). Do not destroy.] As in Psalm lvii. (title).—When Saul sent, etc.] See 1 Sam. 19 : 11–18.

V. 4. Prepare themselves.] For the assault.

V. 5. If all the heathen (first member) are to be visited with his displeasure, much more the revolted and traitors among his own people.

6 They return at evening; they howl like the dog;
And they go round the city.
7 Lo, they belch out with their mouth;
Swords are in their lips;
For who doth hear?
8 But thou, Jehovah, wilt laugh at them;
Thou wilt mock at all the heathen.
9 My strength, I will wait on thee;
For God is my defense.
10 God, with his loving-kindness, will anticipate me;
God will let me see my desire on my enemies.
11 Slay them not, lest my people forget;
Make them reel by thy might, and bring them down,
Our shield, O Lord!
12 A sin of their mouth, is the word of their lips;
And they shall be taken in their pride,
And for cursing, and for the falsehood they tell.
13 Consume in wrath, consume till they are no more;
And let them know that God rules in Jacob,
To the ends of the earth. (*Pause.*)
14 And they will return at evening, will howl like the dog,
And will go round the city.
15 As for them, they will wander about for food;
If they are not sated, they will remain all night.
16 But as for me, I will sing of thy might,
And will sing aloud of thy loving-kindness in the morning.
For thou hast been a tower of defense for me,
And a refuge in the day of my distress.
17 My strength, unto thee will I sing praise;
For God is my defense, my gracious God.

V. 9. My strength.] As in some Hebrew manuscripts, and in ancient versions.

V. 10, 2d member. See the remark on Ps. 54 : 7.

V. 12, 1st member. Meaning: whatever word they utter is sinful; it is a sin of their mouth.

V. 13. Let them know that God rules.] This zeal for the honor of God's government inspires the Psalmist's appeals to his justice.

PSALM LX.

To the chief Musician. After [the melody] "Lily of Testimony." Memorial [Psalm] of David, to be taught; when he strove with Aram Naharaim, and with Aram of Zobah, and Joab returned and smote Edom in the Valley of Salt, twelve thousand.

1 O God, thou hast cast us off, hast scattered us.
Thou wast angry; thou wilt restore to us.
2 Thou hast made the earth quake; thou hast rent it;
Heal the breaches thereof, for it shakes.
3 Thou hast showed thy people a hard thing;
Thou hast made us drink wine even to reeling.
4 Thou hast given to them that fear thee a banner,
To be lifted up because of truth. (*Pause.*)
5 That thy beloved ones may be delivered,
Save with thy right hand and answer me.
6 God has spoken in his holiness. I will triumph;
I will divide Shechem, and will mete out the valley of
Succoth.
7 Gilead is mine, and Manasseh is mine,
And Ephraim is the defense of my head;
Judah is my ruler's staff.

Ps. lx. (title). Lily, the symbol of purity and loveliness; Testimony, the divine law; hence, Beauty of the Divine Law, name of a melody to which this psalm was to be sung.

To be taught.] Namely, the lesson of temporary and partial reverses, (vv. 1–3), with assurance of ultimate triumph through God (vv. 4–12). For a similar direction see Deut. 31 : 19 ("write this song for you, and teach it to the children of Israel"), and 2 Sam. 1 : 18 (properly, "teach the children of Judah The Bow," a song so named from v. 22).

Aram.] Syria.—Aram Naharaim.] Syria of the two rivers (Mesopotamia).

For the historical facts referred to, compare 2 Sam. 8 : 13, 1 Chron. 18 : 12.

Vv. 1–3 seem to refer to reverses in the early conduct of the war, of which only the final triumphs are recorded in history.

V. 3 Hast made us drink wine.] A common expression of the divine displeasure. See, for example, Ps. 75 : 8; Jer. 25 : 15; Rev. 16 : 19.

V. 7. Ruler's staff.] See Gen. 49 : 10 (revised version).

8 Moab is my wash-basin;
Upon Edom will I cast my shoe.
Because of me, Philistia, cry aloud.
9 Who will conduct me to the fenced city?
Who has led me unto Edom?
10 Is it not thou, O God, that didst cast us off,
And goest not forth, O God, with our armies?
11 Give us help from the foe;
For vain is the deliverance of man.
12 Through God we will do valiantly;
And he it is that will tread down our foes.

PSALM LXI.

To the chief Musician. Upon a stringed instrument. [A Psalm] of David.

1 HEAR, O God, my cry;
Attend unto my prayer.
2 From the end of the earth I call to thee when my heart faints.
To a rock, too high for me, thou wilt lead me.
3 For thou hast been a refuge for me,
A tower of strength, from before the enemy.
4 I will abide in thy tabernacle forever;
I will take refuge in the covert of thy wings. (*Pause.*)
5 For thou, O God, hast hearkened to my vows;
Hast given the heritage of them that fear thy name.
6 Thou wilt add days to the days of the king,
His years as many generations.
7 He shall sit [on the throne] before God forever;
Cause that mercy and truth preserve him.
8 So will I sing praise to thy name forever,
That I may perform my vows, day by day.

V. 8, 3d member. *Or*, Over me, Philistia, cry aloud. (Ironical.)

V. 9. Has led me.] Apparently anticipating, and taking for granted, that which he desires and seeks.

V. 2. Too high for me.] That I can not reach without aid.

PSALM LXII.

To the chief Musician over Jeduthun. A Psalm of David.

1 ONLY in God is my soul quieted;
From him is my salvation.
2 Only he is my rock, and my salvation,
My high place; I shall not be greatly moved.
3 How long will ye rush upon a man,
Will ye break him down, all of you,
As a wall inclined, as a fence that is thrust down?
4 They only consult to thrust him from his elevation;
They delight in falsehood.
They bless, each with his mouth, but in their inward part they curse. (*Pause.*)
5 Only in God be thou quieted, my soul;
For from him is my hope.
6 Only he is my rock, and my salvation,
My high place; I shall not be moved.
7 On God [rests] my salvation, and my glory;
The rock of my strength, my refuge, is in God.
8 Trust in him at all times, ye people;
Pour out your heart before him.
God is a refuge for us. (*Pause.*)
9 Only vanity are men of low degree, men of high degree a lie;
In the balances they surely go up;
Together are they less than vanity.
10 Trust not in oppression,
And be not vain in robbery;
When riches increase, set not the heart upon them.
11 Once has God spoken,
Twice have I heard this,
That power belongs to God.
12 And to thee, O Lord, belongs mercy;
For thou wilt render to man according to his work.

Ps. lxii. (title). Jeduthun] A collective, representing the family, or choir, of that name. Compare Ps. xxxix. (title).

PSALM LXIII.

A Psalm of David, when he was in the wilderness of Judah.

1 O God, my God art thou ; earnestly will I seek thee.
My soul thirsts for thee, my flesh pines for thee,
In a land of drought, and fainting, without water.
2 So, in the sanctuary, have I beheld thee,
To see thy power and thy glory.
3 For thy loving-kindness is better than life ;
My lips shall praise thee.
4 So will I bless thee while I live ;
In thy name will I lift up my hands.
5 As with marrow and fatness shall my soul be satisfied,
And my mouth shall praise with joyful lips ;
6 When I remember thee upon by bed,—
In the night-watches I meditate on thee.
7 For thou hast been a help for me,
And in the shadow of thy wings will I rejoice.
8 My soul has followed close upon thee ;
Thy right hand has upheld me.
9 And they, to [their] destruction will they seek my soul ;
They shall go into the depths of the earth.
10 They shall be given over to the power of the sword ;
A portion for jackals shall they be.
11 But the king will rejoice in God ;
They shall glory, every one that swears by him.
For the mouth of them that speak falsehood shall be stopped.

Ps. lxiii. (title). See 2 Sam. 15 : 23, 28.

V. 2. So.] Namely, as I now long to behold thee, that I may see (may apprehend) thy power and thy glory.

V. 6. Night-watches.] Of these there were three ; the "beginning of the watches" (Lam. 2 : 19), the "middle watch" (Judges 7 : 19), the "morning watch" (Ex. 14 : 24).

V. 10. The jackal is common in Palestine, and feeds on bodies of the slain.

V. 11. That swears by him.] Appealing to him as the true God, and a God that delights in truth. See Deut. 6 : 13, Is. 65 : 16 ; and compare Amos 8 : 14.

PSALM LXIV.

To the chief Musician. A Psalm of David.

1 HEAR, O God, my voice in my complaint;
From terror of the enemy thou wilt preserve my life.
2 Thou wilt hide me from the secret counsel of evil-doers,
From the tumultuous throng of workers of iniquity;
3 Who have sharpened their tongue like a sword,
Have fitted their arrow,—bitter speech,
4 To shoot, in the secret places, at the upright.
Suddenly will they shoot at him, and will not fear.
5 They strengthen their evil design;
They concert how to conceal snares.
They have said: Who will look upon them?
6 They search for iniquities;
We are ready [say they]; a device searched out!
And the inward part of each, and the heart, is deep.
7 But God has shot at them;
With an arrow, suddenly, themselves are smitten.
8 And he has made them stumble; their own tongue is against them.
They flee away, every one that looks upon them.
9 And all men feared,
And declared God's doing;
And his work they attentively consider.
10 The righteous will rejoice in Jehovah, and trust in him;
And all the upright in heart will glory.

V. 1. Terror of the enemy.] That which I have reason to dread from him.

V. 5. Strengthen.] Make strong; so frame their malicious plot as to make its success sure.

V. 6. Search for iniquities.] That is, invent, contrive them; as indicated, in the next following line, by their boastful exclamation, "a device searched out!"

V. 8. Their own tongue is against them.] Compare v. 3. Their tongue, which they "have sharpened like a sword" for another's ruin, is now the instrument of their own.

PSALM LXV.

To the chief Musician. A Psalm of David. A Song.

To thee belong submission, praise, O God, in Zion;
And to thee shall the vow be paid.
2 Thou that hearest prayer,
Unto thee shall all flesh come.
3 Iniquities have prevailed over me;
Our transgressions, thou thyself wilt cover them.
4 Happy he whom thou wilt choose and bring near;
He shall dwell in thy courts.
We shall be satisfied with the riches of thy house,
Thy holy temple.
5 By fearful things in righteousness wilt thou answer us,
O God of our salvation,
The confidence of all the ends of earth and sea, afar off;
6 Who sets fast the mountains by his strength,
Girded with power;
7 Who stills the roar of the seas, the roar of their waves,
The tumult of the peoples.
8 Then were they that dwell in the utmost parts afraid at thy tokens.
Thou causest the outgoings of morning and evening to rejoice.
9 Thou hast visited the earth and made it overflow [with plenty];
Thou greatly enrichest it.
The river of God is full of water.
Thou preparest their grain; for so dost thou prepare the earth;

V. 1. To thee belong, etc.] Thou hast a claim, for submission in times of sorrow, for praise in seasons of joy.

V. 4. Riches of thy house.] Its wealth of spiritual blessings.

V. 9. So.] Namely, with this design, and for this end.*

* In the Hebrew, "for so dost thou prepare her;" referring to "the earth," which in Hebrew is fem., while "grain" is masc. The meaning can be expressed in English only by using the word (earth) which the Heb. pronoun represents. The English pronoun (it) would necessarily refer to "grain," and would represent neither the meaning of the Hebrew nor its form.

10 Drenching its furrows, settling its ridges;
Thou makest it soft with showers,
Its springing up thou dost bless.
11 Thou hast crowned the year with thy goodness,
And thy footsteps drip with fatness;
12 The pastures of the wilderness, they drip,
And the hills gird themselves with gladness.
13 The pastures are clothed with flocks,
And the valleys are robed with grain;
They shout together, yea they sing.

PSALM LXVI.

To the chief Musician. A Song. A Psalm.

1 SHOUT unto God, all the earth.
Sing the glory of his name;
2 Ascribe glory, the praise due to him.
3 Say unto God, how fearful are thy doings!
In the greatness of thy strength shall thy enemies profess submission to thee.
4 All the earth shall worship thee,
And shall sing praise to thee;
They shall sing praise to thy name. (*Pause.*)
5 Go, and see the doings of God;
Fearful in action toward the sons of men!
6 He turned the sea into dry land;
They passed through the flood on foot;
There we rejoiced in him.
7 He rules by his might forever.
His eyes keep watch among the nations;
Let not the rebellious exalt themselves. (*Pause.*)
8 Bless our God, ye peoples,
And cause the voice of his praise to be heard;
9 Who holds our soul in life,
And has not suffered our foot to be moved.

V. 6. We rejoiced in him.] Ex. ch. xv.

10 For thou hast tried us, O God;
Thou hast assayed us, as silver is assayed.
11 Thou didst bring us into the net;
Thou didst lay a heavy burden on our loins.
12 Thou didst cause men to ride over our head;
We went through fire and through water;
And thou hast brought us out to overflowing plenty.
13 I will come into thy house with burnt-offerings;
I will pay to thee my vows,
14 Which my lips uttered,
And my mouth spoke, in my distress.
15 Burnt-offerings of fatlings will I offer to thee,
With incense of rams;
I will offer oxen with he-goats. (*Pause.*)
16 Come, hear, and I will declare,
All ye that fear God,
What he has done for my soul.
17 To him I cried with my mouth;
And praise is beneath my tongue.
18 If I regard iniquity in my heart,
The Lord will not hear me.
19 But verily God has heard me;
He has attended to the voice of my prayer.
20 Blessed be God,
Who has not turned away my prayer,
And his mercy from me.

PSALM LXVII.

To the chief Musician. With stringed instruments. A Psalm. A Song.

1 God be gracious to us, and bless us,
Cause his face to shine upon us; (*Pause.*)

V. 17. Beneath my tongue.] Ready for utterance; ever there, and waiting for expression. Compare Ps. 10 : 7, "under his tongue" (in store there).

2 That thy way may be known in the earth,
Thy salvation among all the heathen.
3 Let the peoples praise thee, O God;
Let the peoples praise thee, all of them.
4 Let the nations be glad and shout for joy;
For thou wilt judge the peoples righteously,
And the nations in the earth, thou wilt guide them. (*Pause.*)
5 Let the peoples praise thee, O God;
Let the peoples praise thee, all of them.
6 The earth has yielded her increase;
God, our God, will bless us.
7 God will bless us;
And all the ends of the earth will fear him.

PSALM LXVIII.

To the chief Musician. A Psalm of David. A Song.

1 LET God arise, let his enemies be scattered;
And let them that hate him flee before him.
2 As smoke is driven, thou wilt drive them;
As wax is melted before the fire,
The wicked shall perish before God.
3 But the righteous shall be glad;
They shall exult before God,
And shall rejoice with gladness.
4 Sing to God; sing praise to his name.
Cast up a way for him that rides through the deserts,
By his name, JAH, and triumph before him.

V. 4. Cast up a way.] As a preparation for the march of a king and his armies, over pathless wastes. Compare Is. 40 : 3, 4.

V. 4, 3d member. By his name, Jah.] In the character denoted by it and the power implied in it. This abbreviation of JEHOVAH, frequent in the Psalms, is found in the song of Moses and the children of Israel, Ex. 15 : 2 (properly, "Jah is my strength and song"); and in ch. 17 : 16 (properly Jah, instead of Lord, in the first instance).

5 A father of the orphans, and a judge of the widows,
Is God in his holy habitation.
6 God makes the solitary dwell in families;
He brings out prisoners into prosperity;
But rebels inhabit a parched land.
7 O God, when thou wentest forth before thy people,
When thou didst march through the desert, (*Pause.*)
8 Earth shook, yea, the heavens dropped, at the presence of God,
That Sinai, at the presence of God, the God of Israel.
9 With plentiful rain thou didst sprinkle, O God, thy heritage,
And when fainting, thou thyself hast raised it up.
10 Thy flock, they have dwelt therein;
Thou, O God, dost provide in thy goodness for the poor.
11 The Lord gives the word;
The women that publish the glad tidings are a mighty host.
12 Kings of armies flee, they flee,
And the dweller in the house, she divides the spoil.

V. 6, 1st member. Compare Ps. 113 : 9.

V. 8. The heavens.] The upper air, the region of clouds and storms, as in the following references.—Dropped.] Fell in drops. Compare Judges 5 : 4, "the heavens dropped, yea, the clouds dropped water;" Is. 45 : 8, "drop down ye heavens, from above, and let the skies pour down righteousness."

V. 8, 2d member. That Sinai.] Thus pointed out, as the scene of God's most wonderful manifestation of his presence and authority.

V. 9. *Or*, With a rain of free gifts (namely, manna, etc.).

V. 11. The women that publish the glad tidings.] As in Ex. 15 : 20, ("all the women went out with timbrels"); 1 Sam. 18 : 6 ("the women came out of all the cities of Israel, singing," etc.). VV. 12–14 may be understood to be the message which they proclaim.

Others translate:

Women publish the glad tidings to the mighty host.

In the first member of this verse, "word" may mean, either the word of command to march on the enemy, followed by the triumphant announcement of victory, or the joyful message of victory to be proclaimed.

V. 12. Kings of armies.] Compare Judges 5 : 19, "The kings came and fought."—The dweller in the house.] The housewife.

13 Will ye lie down among the sheepfolds,
The wings of the dove overlaid with silver,
And her feathers with yellow gold?
14 When the Almighty scattered kings therein,
It was snow-white on Salmon.
15 A mount of God is the mount of Bashan;
A mount of peaks is the mount of Bashan.
16 Why watch ye jealously, ye mountain peaks,
The mount which God desired, to dwell in it?
Yea, Jehovah will abide here forever.
17 The chariots of God are myriad-fold, thousands upon thousands;
The Lord is among them—Sinai in the sanctuary!
18 Thou hast ascended on high, hast led captive the captured,
Hast taken gifts among men,
And even rebels, that Jah, God, may abide here.
19 Blessed be the Lord, day by day;
He bears our burden; God is our salvation. (*Pause.*)

V. 13. A sharp remonstrance. Will ye lie at ease, in the quiet of your pastoral life, as the dove with unsoiled plumage in her peaceful nest, while your brethren are in the tumult and dust of the conflict! Compare Judges 5:16 (from which this allusion is taken) and 17.

V. 14. Salmon] Probably an eminence in the vicinity of Shechem. Snow-white.] With the bones of the slain.

V. 15. A mount of God.] Denoting what is greatest and noblest of its kind. A mount of peaks, a mountain range with many lofty summits. These are conceived as jealously watching the more humble eminence, which God has distinguished above them by choosing it for his abode.

V. 17. Myriad-fold.] Compared with those of the enemy. Compare 2 Kings 6:17.

V. 17. Sinai in the sanctuary.] In the sanctuary is repeated the scene of Sinai, where Jehovah appeared, as he now does here, with "myriads of holy ones" (Deut. 33:2).

V. 18. Hast led captive the captured.] That is, hast led the captured as captives, in the train of the victor. Compare Judges 5:12, properly, "lead thy captured captive."

V. 18. Gifts.] Exacted of the vanquished by the conqueror.

V. 18. Abide here.] Compare v. 16, 3d member.

20 God is to us a God for deliverances;
And to Jehovah the Lord belong ways of escape from death.
21 Surely God will crush the head of his enemies,
The hairy crown of him that goes on in his trespasses.
22 The Lord has said: From Bashan will I bring back,
I will bring back from the depths of the sea;
23 That thy foot may bathe in blood,
The tongue of thy dogs have its portion from the enemies.
24 They saw thy goings, O God,
The goings of my God, my king, in the sanctuary.
25 Before went singers, behind, players on stringed instruments,
In the midst of maidens beating timbrels.
26 In companies they bless God,
The Lord, they that are of Israel's fountain.
27 There is little Benjamin, their ruler;
Princes of Judah, their multitude;
Princes of Zebulon, princes of Naphtali.
28 Thy God has commanded thy strength;
Strengthen, O God, what thou hast wrought for us.
29 Because of thy temple at Jerusalem,
Kings shall bring presents to thee.
30 Rebuke the beast of the reeds,
The herd of bullocks, with the calves of the peoples,
Prostrating themselves with pieces of silver.
He has scattered peoples that delight in wars.
31 Princes shall come out of Egypt;
Ethiopia shall eagerly stretch out her hands to God.

V. 24. Goings.] Solemn processions, on account of victory over the enemy, or other occasions of gratitude and rejoicing.

V. 27. There.] In the triumphal procession, the description of which commences with v. 24.—Their ruler.] An ancient prophetic idea. Compare Mic. 5:2.

V. 30. Beast of the reeds.] Egypt, designated by one of its characteristic representatives in the animal kingdom. Compare Job 40:21.

V. 30, 2d member. Bullocks.] The strong ones of the people, their leaders.—Calves of the peoples.] The weaker ones, the common people.

V. 30, 3d member. With pieces of silver.] As tribute money for the conqueror.

32 Kingdoms of the earth, sing unto God;
Sing praises to the Lord; (*Pause.*)
33 To him that rides in the heavens of heavens of old.
Lo, he utters his voice, a mighty voice.
34 Ascribe strength to God.
Over Israel is his majesty,
And his strength in the clouds.
35 Terrible art thou, O God, out of thy holy places,
Mighty One of Israel;
He that gives strength and peace to the people.
Blessed be God!

PSALM LXIX.

To the chief Musician. To [the melody] "Lilies." [A Psalm] of David.

1 SAVE me, O God,
For the waters have come in, even to the soul.
2 I am sunk in mire of the deep, and there is no standing-place.
I am come into the depths of waters,
And the flood has overwhelmed me.
3 I am weary with my crying, my throat is parched;
My eyes fail, while I wait for my God.
4 More than the hairs of my head are they that hate me without cause;
Strong are they that would destroy me, my enemies wrongfully.
What I took not away, must I then restore.
5 O God, thou knowest as to my foolishness,
And my trespasses have not been hidden from thee.
6 Let not them be ashamed in me, that wait for thee,
O Lord, Jehovah of hosts.
Let not them be dishonored in me, that seek thee,
O God of Israel.

V. 4, 3d member. Then.] In that case, though I took it not, as falsely charged.

V. 6. In me.] As representing them all.

7 Because for thy sake I have borne reproach ;
Shame has covered my face.
8 I am become a stranger to my brethren,
And an alien to the sons of my mother.
9 For zeal for thy house consumed me,
And the reproaches of them that reproached thee fell on me.
10 And I wept, while my spirit fasted,
And it was a reproach to me.
11 And I made sackcloth my garment,
And I became a by-word to them.
12 They talk of me, they that sit in the gate,
And the songs of the drinkers of strong drink.
13 But as for me, my prayer is to thee, O Jehovah ;
At a time of acceptance, O God, in the abundance of thy mercy,
Answer me in the truth of thy salvation.
14 Rescue me out of the mire, and let me not sink ;
Let me be rescued from them that hate me,
And from the depths of waters.
15 Let not the flood of waters overwhelm me,
And let not the deep swallow me up,
And let not the pit shut her mouth upon me.
16 Answer me, O Jehovah, for thy loving-kindness is good ;
According to the multitude of thy compassions turn unto me.
17 And do not hide thy face from thy servant ;
For I am in trouble,—make haste to answer me.
18 Draw nigh to my soul, redeem it ;
Because of my enemies deliver me.
19 Thou dost know my reproach, and my shame, and my dishonor ;
All my adversaries are before thee.
20 Reproach has broken my heart, and I am sick ;
And I looked for pity, but there was none,
And for comforters, but I found none.

V. 13, 3d member. The truth of thy salvation.] The salvation of God is truth and fidelity, on his part, to those who trust in him. He "is faithful and just to forgive" (1 John 1 : 9).

21 And they put gall in my food,
And for my thirst they gave me vinegar to drink.
22 Let their table before them be for a snare,
And to the secure for a trap.
23 Let their eyes be darkened, that they may not see,
And make their loins waver continually.
24 Pour upon them thine indignation,
And let the heat of thine anger overtake them.
25 Let their habitation be desolated,
Let there be no dweller in their tents.
26 For whom thou hast smitten they persecute,
And tell of the pain of thy wounded.
27 Add iniquity to their iniquity,
And let them not come into thy righteousness.
28 Let them be blotted from the book of life,
And with the righteous let them not be written.
29 And I am afflicted and sorrowful;
Thy salvation, O God, shall set me on high.
30 I will praise the name of God in song,
And will magnify him with thanksgiving.

V. 22. Their table before them.] At which they sit, feasting and suspecting no evil. So in the next member, "to the secure," apprehending no danger.

VV. 22–28. It has been well said by Dr. Alexander (on this passage) that these imprecations are "revolting only when considered as the expression of malignant selfishness. If uttered by God, they shock no reader's sensibilities, nor should they when considered as the language of an ideal person, representing the whole class of righteous sufferers, and particularly HIM, who, though he prayed for his murderers while dying (Luke 23 : 34), had applied the words of this passage to the unbelieving Jews (Matt. 23 : 38), as Paul did afterward (Rom. 11 : 9, 10)." See a full and satisfactory discussion of the subject in the article "Imprecatory Psalms" (added to the art. Psalms, in the American edition of *Smith's Bible Dictionary*), especially division (v).

V. 27. As each new act of iniquity is committed, add it to the former sum.

V. 27, 2d member. Let them not come into thy righteousness.] Let them have no participation in it.

V. 28, 1st member. *Or*, from the book of the living.

31 It will better please Jehovah than an ox, a bullock,
With horns, with cloven hoofs.
32 The humble have seen it; they will rejoice.
Seekers of God, let your hearts revive!
33 For Jehovah hearkens to the needy,
And his prisoners he has not despised.
34 Let the heavens and the earth praise him,
The seas, and everything that moves therein.
35 For God will save Zion,
And will build the cities of Judah;
And they dwell there, and shall possess it.
36 And the seed of his servants shall inherit it,
And they that love his name shall abide therein.

PSALM LXX.

To the chief Musician. [A Psalm] of David. To bring to remembrance.

1 O God,—to my rescue,
O Jehovah,—to my help make haste.
2 They shall be ashamed and confounded that seek my soul;
They shall be turned back and put to confusion that delight in my harm.
3 They shall turn back for a reward of their shame,
Who say, Aha! Aha!
4 They shall rejoice and be glad in thee, all that seek thee;
And they shall say always, God be magnified,
That love thy salvation.
5 And I am afflicted and needy;
O God, make haste to me.
My help and my deliverer art thou;
O Jehovah, do not delay!

V. 31. With cloven hoofs.] All others accounted unclean (Lev. 13:3–8).

PSALM LXXI.

1 In thee, Jehovah, I put my trust;
Let me not be ashamed, forevermore.
2 In thy righteousness thou wilt rescue me, and deliver me;
Incline to me thine ear, and save me.
3 Be thou to me a rock of refuge, to come thither continually.
Thou hast commanded to save me,
For my rock and my fortress art thou.
4 My God, deliver me from the hand of the wicked,
From the grasp of the perverse and violent.
5 For thou art my hope,
O Lord, Jehovah, my trust from my youth.
6 On thee have I been sustained from the womb;
Thou art he that took me from the bowels of my mother.
Of thee is my praise continually.
7 As a wonder have I been to many;
But thou art my strong refuge.
8 My mouth shall be filled with thy praise,
With thy majesty, all the day.
9 Cast me not away at the time of old age;
As my strength fails, do not forsake me.
10 For my enemies have said it of me;
And they that watch for my soul have counseled together,
11 Saying: God has forsaken him,
Pursue and take him, for there is none to rescue.
12 O God, be not far from me;
My God, make haste to my help.
13 They shall be ashamed, shall consume away, that are adversaries of my soul;
They shall be covered with reproach and dishonor that seek my harm.
14 But I, continually will I hope,
And will add to all thy praise.

V. 14. Will add to all thy praise.] Shall have further occasions to praise thee, in addition to all in the past.

15 My mouth shall recount thy righteousness,
Thy salvation all the day,
For I know not the numbers.
16 I will come with the mighty deeds of the Lord Jehovah;
I will make mention of thy righteousness, thine only.
17 O God, thou hast taught me from my youth;
And hitherto do I make known thy wondrous works.
18 And even to old age, and hoary hairs, O God, do not forsake me;
Till I shall make known thine arm to generations,
Thy might to every one that is to come.
19 And thy righteousness, O God, is even unto the height,
Thou who hast done great things.
O God, who is like to thee?
20 Thou, who hast made us see troubles great and sore,
Wilt again revive us,
And from the abysses of the earth wilt bring us up again.
21 Thou wilt increase my greatness, and wilt turn again to comfort me.
22 I too will praise thee, with an instrument, a lute,
Thy truth, O my God;
I will sing praise to thee with the harp, thou Holy One of Israel.
23 My lips shall rejoice, for I will sing praise to thee,
And my soul, which thou hast redeemed.
24 Also my tongue all the day shall speak of thy righteousness;
For they are confounded, they are brought to shame, that seek my harm.

V. 16. I will come.] Into thy house; as in Ps. 42 : 2, "When shall I come, and appear before God?" Compare Ps. 66 : 13. There it is said, "I will come into thy house with burnt-offerings;" here, "with the mighty deeds of the Lord Jehovah" (the thankful recognition of them).

V. 19. The height.] The summit, the highest point; here equivalent to the heavens. Compare the sentiment in Ps. 57 : 10, "Great, unto the heavens, is thy mercy."

V. 20. Abysses of the earth.] Abysses of water within the earth, conceived as the exhaustless source of streams that issue on its surface. See Gen. 49 : 25, "the abyss that lies under;" Deut. 8 : 7, properly, "and

PSALM LXXII.

[A Psalm] of Solomon.

1 O God, give to the king thy judgments,
And thy righteousness to the king's son.
2 He shall judge thy people with righteousness,
And thy poor with rectitude.
3 The mountains shall bear peace for the people,
And the hills, by righteousness.
4 He shall judge the poor of the people ;
He shall save the sons of the needy ;
He shall break in pieces the oppressor.
5 They shall fear thee while the sun endures,
As long as the moon, to all generations.
6 He shall come down as rain upon the mown grass,
As showers that refresh the earth.
7 In his days shall the righteous flourish,
And abundance of peace, till the moon be no more.
8 And he shall rule from sea to sea,
And from the river to the ends of the earth.
9 They of the desert shall crouch before him,
And his enemies shall lick the dust.
10 Kings of Tarshish and the isles shall bring presents ;
Kings of Sheba and Seba shall offer gifts.
11 And all kings shall bow down to him ;
All nations shall serve him.
12 For he will rescue the needy, crying for help,
The poor, and him that has no helper.
13 He will have pity on the weak and needy,
And will save the souls of the needy.
14 From extortion and from violence he will redeem their soul ;
And precious is their blood in his eyes.

---

of abysses issuing forth in valley and in mountain ;" 33 : 13, properly, "the abyss lying beneath."

V. 1. Give to the king, etc.] Confer upon him, along with the powers of a sovereign ruler, the qualifications for duly exercising them. The thought, in both members of this verse, is expanded in Is. 11 : 2–4.

15 And he shall live; and will give to him of the gold of Sheba,
And will pray for him continually;
All the day will he bless him.
16 There shall be abundance of grain in the land;
On the top of the mountains its fruit shall wave like Lebanon;
And they shall bloom forth from the city like the herb of the earth.
17 His name shall be forever;
As long as the sun shall his name flourish.
And in him shall they bless themselves;
All nations shall call him happy.
18 Blessed be Jehovah God, the God of Israel,
Who alone doeth wonders.
19 And blessed be his glorious name forevermore;
And let the whole earth be filled with his glory.

AMEN, AND AMEN.

The prayers of David the Son of Jesse are ended.

V. 15. He.] The redeemed.

V. 16, 3d member. Shall bloom forth from the city (the cities as centres of population), multiplying like the herb of the earth.

THIRD BOOK.

PSALM LXXIII.

A Psalm of Asaph.

1 SURELY, God is good to Israel,
To the pure in heart.
2 And as for me, my feet almost turned aside ;
My steps well-nigh slid.
3 For I was envious at the foolish,
When I saw the prosperity of the wicked.
4 For their death has no pains,
And their strength is full fed.
5 In the troubles of men they share not,
And they are not plagued in common with men.
6 Therefore pride is become their necklace ;
The garb of violence covers them.
7 Their eyes stand out with fatness ;
They have more than heart conceives.
8 They mock, and with malice they speak oppression ;
From on high they speak.
9 They have set their mouth in the heavens,
And their tongue walks through the earth.

V. 6. Pride is become their necklace.] The lofty neck of pride is meant, the natural indication of a haughty and supercilious spirit. Pride encircles it as does a necklace.

V. 8. They speak oppression.] Their word is power. They have only to speak, and their oppressive will is done.

10 Therefore do his people turn away hither,
And waters in abundance are eagerly drained by them.
11 And they say: How does God know?
And is there knowledge in the Most High?
12 Behold, such are the wicked;
And forever secure they have increased wealth.
13 Surely, in vain have I cleansed my heart,
And washed my hands in innocency;
14 And been smitten all the day long,
My chastisement morning by morning.
15 If I say, I will declare thus,
Behold, I should deal falsely with the generation of thy children.
16 And I meditated to know this;
It was an evil in my eyes;
17 Till I went in to the sanctuary of God,—
Gave heed to their end.
18 Surely, thou dost set them in slippery places;
Thou dost cast them down to ruin.
19 How are they brought to desolation as in a moment!
They are swept away, they are consumed with terrors.
20 As a dream when one awakes,
O Lord, when thou awakest, thou dost despise their image.
21 For my heart is embittered,
And I am pierced in my reins.

V. 10. The sense appears to be: Therefore do his people (God's people) turn away hither (from the right way into these forbidden ways, where they see others prospering), and find a full supply (waters in abundance). In the next following verse this practical atheism finds expression in words.

V. 15. If I say.] Purpose in my heart.—Declare thus.] Make known these perplexing doubts.

V. 20. Their image.] Their pomp of pride and power; as unsubstantial, and as despicable in the sight of God, when he awakes to deal with them, as is a dream of the night, after awaking.

V. 21. For.] Resuming the thought from vv. 16, 17, and his state of mind there referred to, as an introduction to the just condemnation of himself in v. 22.

22 And I am brutish, and know not;
A beast have I been before thee.
23 But I am continually with thee;
Thou hast kept hold of my right hand.
24 Thou wilt guide me by thy counsel,
And afterward wilt receive me to glory.
25 Whom have I in heaven?
And with thee I have no delight on the earth.
26 My strength and my heart fail;
The rock of my heart and my portion is God forevermore.
27 For lo, they that are far from thee shall perish;
Thou hast destroyed all that adulterously forsake thee.
28 And as for me, to draw near to God is good for me.
I have made the Lord Jehovah my refuge,
That I may tell of all thy works.

PSALM LXXIV.

Didactic [Psalm] of Asaph.

1 WHEREFORE, O God, hast thou cast off forever?
Why does thine anger smoke against the sheep of thy pasture?
2 Remember thy congregation thou didst purchase of old,
Didst redeem as the tribe of thine inheritance,
This mount Zion wherein thou hast dwelt.

V. 25. With thee.] Either, with thee for my own, that is, having thee; or, along with thee, in addition to thee.

V. 26. The rock of my heart.] Its firm and unfailing support.

V. 27. Adulterously forsake thee.] Representing God's spiritual relation to his chosen people by that of the husband to the wife (compare Jer. 3 : 14, "for I am married to you"), and idolatry as unfaithfulness to that relation.

V. 2. Tribe of thine inheritance.] Compare Is. 63 : 17, "the tribes of thine inheritance."

The words may be rendered (in the same general sense), a people for thy possession. The same expression occurs in the New Testament;

3 Lift thy steps to the perpetual ruins,
All that the enemy has wickedly done in the sanctuary.
4 Thine adversaries have roared in the midst of thine assembly;
Their ensigns they have set for signs.
5 It seems as when one lifts up axes,
In the thicket of the wood;
6 So now all the carved work thereof
With axe and hammers they beat down.
7 They have set on fire thy sanctuary;
To the ground have they profaned the dwelling-place of thy name.
8 They said in their heart: Let us destroy them together;
They have burned all God's places of assembly in the land.
9 Our signs we see not;
There is no prophet any more,
Nor is there any among us that knows how long.
10 How long, O God, shall the foe reproach?
Shall the enemy contemn thy name forever?

Tit. 2 : 14, "and cleanse for himself a people for a possession" (Revised Version, "a people to be his own"); 1 Pet. 2 : 9 (Revised Version correctly, "a people for a possession").

V. 4. Have roared.] Like wild beasts.

V. 4, 2d member. Their ensigns.] Their banners, as the Hebrew word is used in Num. 2 : 2.

For signs.] Tokens to them of triumph and conquest; to us, of humiliation and abandonment by God. Compare v. 9.

The same Hebrew word is here rendered *ensign* and *sign*, having both these senses. Some would translate, Their signs they have set for signs. "Their signs" meaning either the marks of their ravages, or their idolatrous images, or their unholy rites, or all these. "They have set for signs," in the sense above given.*

V. 5. Their ravages are as reckless and destructive as the woodman's axe in the forest.

V. 8. God's places of assembly.] For religious instruction and devotion, not for services peculiar to the temple.

* To the Hebrew mind the two applications of the word "sign" would be very obvious, though it would not suggest itself to us; and the rendering in the text is probably the true expression of the sense.

11 Wherefore dost thou withdraw thy hand, even thy right hand?
Forth from the midst of thy bosom destroy!
12 And God is my king of old,
Working deliverances in the earth.
13 Thou didst cleave the sea by thy strength;
Didst break the heads of monsters on the waters.
14 Thou didst crush the heads of leviathan,
Didst give him for food to them that people the desert.
15 Thou didst break open the fountain and brook;
Thou didst dry up ever-flowing streams.
16 Thine is the day, yea night is thine;
Thou hast prepared the light and sun.
17 Thou hast set all the bounds of the earth;
Summer and winter,—thou hast formed them.
18 Remember this, an enemy has reproached Jehovah,
And a foolish people have contemned thy name.
19 Do not give over to the greedy herd thy turtle-dove;
The congregation of thy poor do not forget forever.
20 Have respect to the covenant;
For the dark places of the earth are full of the habitations of cruelty.
21 Let not the oppressed turn back ashamed;
Let the poor and needy praise thy name.

V. 11. Forth from the midst of thy bosom.] Whence the destroying force, now reposing inactive there, shall be drawn forth.

V. 13. Didst cleave the sea.] Ex. 14 : 21.

V. 14. Leviathan.*] A general name for reptiles and fishes of monstrous size; as the serpent (or dragon) Is. 27 : 1, Job 3 : 8; the crocodile Job 41 : 1; a sea-monster (the whale, for example) Ps. 104 : 26. As the crocodile, it here symbolizes Egypt (compare the similar case in Ps. 68 : 30) and the representatives of its power, whose bodies were given for food (next verse) to beasts of prey that peopled the desert. Compare Ex. 14 : 30.

V. 14, 2d member. That people the desert.] Beasts of prey.

V. 15, 1st member. See Num. 20 : 11, and compare Is. 48 : 21.

V. 15, 2d member. See Ex. 14 : 27 (properly, returned to its ceaseless flowing), and Josh. 3 : 16, 17.

* Here for the class to which the individual belongs, with the effect of a plural.

22 Arise, O God, plead thine own cause;
Remember thou art reproached by the fool daily.
23 Do not forget the voice of thine adversaries,
The noise of them that rise against thee, ascending continually.

PSALM LXXV.

To the chief Musician. Do not Destroy. A Psalm of Asaph. A Song

1 WE give thanks to thee, O God, we give thanks;
And that thy name is near, thy wonders have told.
2 For I will take a set time;
I, I will judge equitably.
3 The earth and all that dwell in it are dissolving;
I, I bear up its pillars. (*Pause.*)
4 I said to the fools: Do not deal foolishly,
And to the wicked: Do not lift up the horn.
5 Do not lift up on high your horn,
Nor speak with a stiff neck.
6 For not from the east, and not from the west,
And not from the south, is promotion.
7 For God is judge;
He puts down one, and raises up another.

Ps. lxxv. (title). Do not destroy.] See the remark on Ps. lvii. (title).

V. 1. Near.] For help; a present God, ever at hand, to be invoked in the moment of need. Deut. 4 : 7.

V. 3. Dissolving.] Melting away, sinking into ruin; a picture of social and political disorder and dissolution.

V. 3, 2d member. I bear up its pillars.] I maintain order and peace. It is common to regard vv. 2 and 3 (and some include the following one) as the language of the Almighty, abruptly introduced as speaking, as in Ps. 46 : 10. But it is also appropriate language for the magistrate, to whom it belongs, as God's representative, to maintain civil and social order, as well as for one speaking in his name, and on his behalf. Compare v. 10.

V. 4. Horn.] The symbol of strength, and also of pride and insolent defiance. To lift up the horn of any one (v. 10) means to strengthen him, and add to his power and dignity.

8 For in the hand of Jehovah is a cup,
And it foams with wine, full of mixture ;
And he pours out thereof.
Yea, its dregs they shall wring out, shall drink,
All the wicked of the earth.
9 But I, I will make known forever ;
I will sing praise to the God of Jacob.
10 And all the horns of the wicked will I cut off ;
The horns of the righteous shall be lifted up.

PSALM LXXVI.

To the chief Musician. On stringed instruments. A Psalm of Asaph. A Song.

1 In Judah is God known ;
His name is great in Israel.
2 And in Salem was his tabernacle,
And his dwelling-place in Zion.
3 There broke he the arrows of the bow,
Shield, and sword, and war. (*Pause.*)
4 Resplendent art thou, glorious,
More than the mountains of prey.
5 The strong of heart were despoiled ;
They have slept their sleep,
And none of the men of might found their hands.

V. 8. Mixture.] Of spices and wine, to increase its intoxicating power.

Ps. lxxvi. is one of the most animated of the many psalms written in commemoration of the great deliverance recorded in Is. 37 : 33–36.

V. 3. Hebrew, lightnings of the bow ; a poetical term for the arrow, expressive of its swiftness and destructive force.

V. 4. Mountains of prey.] The abode of beasts of prey ; in their wild magnificence combining grandeur and sublimity with dread.

V. 5. Found their hands.] Found the use of them, were able to employ them in defense ; so sudden and unlooked for, and so inevitable, was the destruction. Compare the similar phrase in 2 Sam. 7 : 27 (properly, found heart to pray this prayer).

6 At thy rebuke, O God of Jacob,
They lay in deep sleep, both chariot and horse.
7 Thou, terrible art thou;
And who may stand before thee when once thou art angry?
8 From heaven thou didst cause judgment to be heard;
Earth feared, and was still,
9 When God arose to judgment,
To save all the humble of the earth. (*Pause.*)
10 For the wrath of man shall praise thee,
The remnant of wrath thou girdest on.
11 Vow, and pay to Jehovah your God;
Let all that are about him bring gifts to him that should be feared.
12 He cuts off the spirit of princes;
He is terrible to the kings of the earth.

PSALM LXXVII.

To the chief Musician over Jeduthun. A Psalm of Asaph.

1 My voice is unto God, and I will cry;
My voice is unto God, and do thou give ear to me.
2 In the day of my distress I sought the Lord;
My hand by night was stretched out, and slackened not.
My soul refused to be comforted.
3 I call God to mind, and sigh;
I lament, and my spirit faints. (*Pause.*)
4 Thou hast held my eyes waking,
I am disquieted, and can not speak.
5 I thought on the days of old,
The years of ancient times.

V. 6. Lay in deep sleep.] Compare, on vv. 5, 6, Is. 37 : 36.

V. 8. Was still.] With awe and dread.

V. 10. Thou girdest on.] As a weapon. Even to the last remnant, it shall serve as part of the armory of God.

Ps. lxxvii. (title). Over Jeduthun]. See the remark on Ps. lxii. (title).

V. 2. Slackened not.] Was unwearied in the attitude of supplication.

6 I call to mind my song in the night;
I commune with my heart,
And my spirit makes search.
7 Will the Lord cast off forever?
And will he favor no more?
8 Has his mercy ceased forever?
Has the promise failed to all generations?
9 Has the Mighty One forgotten to be gracious,
Or in anger shut up his tender mercies? (*Pause.*)
10 And I said: This is my infirmity!
Years of the right hand of the Most High
11 Will I commemorate,—the deeds of Jah.
For I will remember thy wonders from of old;
12 And I will meditate on all thy work,
And think on all thy doings.
13 O God, in holiness is thy way;
Who is a Mighty One, great like God?
14 Thou art the Mighty One, doing wonders;
Thou hast made known thy strength among the peoples.
15 Thou hast redeemed with the arm thy people,
The sons of Jacob and Joseph. (*Pause.*)
16 The waters saw thee, O God;
The waters saw thee, they trembled;
Yea, the depths quaked.
17 The clouds poured out water;
The skies uttered a voice;
Yea, thine arrows went abroad.
18 The voice of thy thunder rolled along;
Lightnings lightened the world;
The earth quaked and shook.

V. 6. My song in the night.] In former experiences of the divine favor.—Makes search.] For an answer to the questions that follow.

V. 8. The promise.] To the chosen seed, many times repeated.

V. 11. Jah.] See the note on Ps. 68 : 5.

V. 15. *Pause.*] See the remark on Ps. 3 : 2. "The music here comes in, and the whole strophe (vv. 13–15) is an overture to the following hymn to God, the Deliverer from Egypt." (*Delitzsch,* on the passage.)

VV. 16–20. Ex. 14 : 19–31.

19 Thy way was in the sea,
And thy paths in great waters,
And thy footsteps were not known.
20 Thou didst guide thy people like a flock,
By the hand of Moses and Aaron.

PSALM LXXVIII.

Didactic [Psalm] of Asaph.

1 GIVE ear, my people, to my law;
Incline your ear to the sayings of my mouth.
2 I will open my mouth in a parable;
I will utter dark sayings from of old.
3 What we have heard, and have known,
And our fathers have told us,
4 We will not hide from their children;
Recounting to after generations the praises of Jehovah,
And his might, and his wonders which he wrought.
5 For he set up a testimony in Jacob,
And appointed a law in Israel;
Which he commanded our fathers,
To make them known to their sons.
6 To the end that after generations might know;
Sons might be born,
Might arise and tell to their sons;
7 And might place in God their hope,
And not forget the deeds of the Mighty One,
And might keep his commandments;
8 And not be as their fathers,
A stubborn and rebellious generation;
A generation that was not steadfast in their heart,
And their spirit was not truthful with God.
9 The sons of Ephraim, armed bowmen,
Turned back in the day of conflict.

V. 9. Sons of Ephraim.] Representing the kingdom of the revolted ten tribes.

V. 9, 2d member. Turned back.] From the conflict to be waged for the extermination of idolatry from the land.

10 They kept not the covenant of God,
And in his law they refused to walk.
11 And they forgot his deeds,
And his wonders which he showed them.
12 In the sight of their fathers he wrought wonders,
In the land of Egypt, the plain of Zoan.
13 He divided the sea, and let them pass through;
And he made the waters stand as a heap.
14 And he guided them in the cloud by day,
And every night in the light of fire.
15 He clave rocks in the wilderness,
And gave them water as the depths, abundantly.
16 And he brought flowing streams out of the cliff,
And made waters run down like rivers.
17 And they continued still to sin against him,
To rebel against the Most High in the desert.
18 And they tempted God in their heart,
So as to ask food for their greediness.
19 And they spoke against God;
They said: Is the Mighty One able
To spread a table in the wilderness?
20 Lo, he smote the rock, and the waters flowed,
And streams gushed out.
Will he also be able to give bread,
Or will he provide flesh for his people?
21 Therefore, Jehovah heard and was wroth;
And fire was kindled in Jacob,
And also anger rose up against Israel;
22 Because they did not believe in God,
And trusted not in his deliverance.
23 And he commanded the skies above,
And the doors of heaven he opened;

V. 12. Zoan.] See the writer's remark on Gen. 12 : 15, second paragraph.

V. 14. His presence in the cloud, and in the pillar of fire (Ex. 13 : 21, 22), was their guide.

V. 15. Clave rocks.] Ex. 17 : 6; Num. 20 : 8–11.

V. 16. Out of the cliff.] As properly translated, Num. 20 : 8.

24 And rained upon them manna for food,
And grain of heaven he gave them.
25 Bread of the mighty did man eat;
He sent them provision in abundance.
26 He caused an east-wind to blow in the heavens,
And led by his strength a south-wind.
27 And he rained flesh upon them as the dust,
And winged fowl as the sand of the seas;
28 And let them fall in the midst of his encampment,
Round about his dwellings.
29 And they ate and were fully satisfied,
And he brought them their desire.
30 They were not estranged from their desire,—
Their food was yet in their mouths,—
31 And the anger of God came up against them,
And he slew among the stoutest of them,
And Israel's young men he brought low.
32 For all this, they still sinned,
And believed not in his wonders.
33 And he consumed their days in vanity,
And their years in terror.
34 If he slew them, then they sought him,
And returned, and eagerly inquired after God.
35 And they remembered that God was their rock,
And the Mighty One, the Most High, their redeemer.
36 But they deceived him with their mouth,
And with their tongue they lied to him;
37 And their heart was not steadfast with him,
And they were not truthful to his covenant.

V. 25. The mighty.] Angels are meant, who are called "mighty in strength," Ps. 103 : 20.

V. 30. Not estranged from their desire.] Not yet satisfied with food; it was still in their mouths (next member).

V. 32. Believed not in his wonders.] Saw in them no ground of faith and trust for the future. Compare Num. 14 : 11.

V. 33. Consumed, etc.] During the long and fruitless wanderings and perils in the desert.

38 But he, the compassionate, covers iniquity, and destroys not;
And many times he turned away his anger,
And would not rouse up all his wrath.
39 For he remembered that they were flesh,—
A breath, that goes, and returns not.
40 How oft they rebelled against him in the wilderness,
Grieved him in the desert!
41 And they tempted God anew,
And offended the Holy One of Israel.
42 They remembered not his hand,
The day when he redeemed them from the foe;
43 When he set his signs in Egypt,
And his portents in the plain of Zoan;
44 And turned their rivers into blood,
And their streams they could not drink.
45 He sent among them flies, and they devoured them,
And frogs, and they desolated them.
46 And he gave their increase to the caterpillar,
And their labor to the locust.
47 He killed their vines with hail,
And their sycamores with frost;
48 And delivered up their cattle to the hail,
And their herds to the lightnings.
49 He cast upon them the burning of his anger,
Wrath, and indignation, and anguish,
An embassy of angels of evil.

V. 43. Set his signs.] Not simply wrought wonders, but set them as signs, as permanent memorials, of his presence and power. Set his signs, therefore, expresses not a passing act, but something abiding and permanent—Portents.] See the remark on Ps. 105 : 5.

VV. 49, 50. These remarkable lines introduce the last great plague; when, "at midnight, Jehovah smote all the firstborn of Egypt, from the firstborn of Pharaoh that sat on his throne, to the firstborn of the captive in the dungeon, and all the firstborn of cattle;" "and there was a great cry in Egypt, for there was not a house where there was not one dead." (Ex. 12 : 29, 30.) This was, truly, "an embassy of angels of evil;" and well is it said, that Jehovah "leveled a path for his anger." It had free course.

50 He leveled a path for his anger.
He withheld not their soul from death,
And their life he delivered up to the plague.
51 And he smote every firstborn in Egypt,
The firstlings of strength in the tents of Ham.
52 And he removed, as a flock, his own people,
And guided them, as a herd, in the wilderness;
53 And he led them on safely, and they feared not,
But their enemies the sea overwhelmed.
54 And he brought them to his holy border,
This mountain, which his right hand won.
55 And he drove out nations before them,
And allotted them an inheritance by line,
And caused the tribes of Israel to dwell in their tents.
56 And they tempted and rebelled against God, Most High,
And his testimonies they did not keep.
57 And they turned back, and dealt falsely like their fathers;
They turned aside like a deceitful bow.
58 And they provoked his displeasure with their high places,
And moved him to jealousy with their graven images.
59 God heard, and was wroth,
And greatly abhorred Israel.
60 And he rejected the dwelling at Shiloh,
The tabernacle which he set up among men;
61 And gave up to captivity his strength,
And his glory into the hand of the foe.
62 And he delivered up his people to the sword,
And was wroth with his inheritance.

V. 52. Removed, as a flock.] As the shepherd removes his flock, from one place of encampment and pasturage to another.

V. 54. Border.] By this is here meant the whole circuit of the holy land, with all that it inclosed.

V. 55. Allotted.] Josh. 13 : 6, "divide thou it by lot to the Israelites for an inheritance."—By line.] Measuring line. For this practice, compare Am. 7 : 17.

V. 60. 2d member. See Josh. 18 : 1.

V. 61. See 1 Sam. 4 : 17.

63 His young men fire consumed,
And his maidens were not praised.
64 His priests fell by the sword,
And his widows wept not.
65 And the Lord awaked, as one that slept;
As a mighty man jubilant with wine.
66 And he smote back his foes,
He laid upon them eternal reproach.
67 And he rejected the tabernacle of Joseph;
And the tribe of Ephraim he did not choose.
68 And he chose the tribe of Judah,
The Mount Zion which he loved.
69 And he built his sanctuary as the heights of heaven,
As the earth which he founded forever.
70 And he chose David his servant,
And took him from the sheepfolds.
71 From following the suckling ewes he took him,
To be shepherd over Jacob his people,
And over Israel his inheritance.
72 And he fed them after the integrity of his heart,
And by the skillfulness of his hands he led them.

PSALM LXXIX.

A Psalm of Asaph.

1 O God, the heathen have come into thy inheritance;
They have defiled thy holy temple;
They have made Jerusalem heaps.
2 They have made the dead bodies of thy servants
Food for the fowls of heaven,
The flesh of thy saints for the beasts of the earth.

V. 63. Fire.] Of desolating war. Num. 21 : 28; Is. 26 : 11; Jer. 48 : 45.

V. 63, 2d member. Were not praised.] In nuptial songs. None were given in marriage.

3 They have shed their blood like water,
Round about Jerusalem, and there is none to bury.
4 We have become a contempt to our neighbors,
A scorn and derision to those around us.
5 How long, O Jehovah! Wilt thou be angry forever?
Will thy jealousy burn like fire?
6 Pour out thy wrath upon the heathen who know thee not,
And upon the kingdoms that call not on thy name.
7 For they have devoured Jacob,
And have laid waste his dwelling-place.
8 Remember not against us the iniquities of the forefathers.
Haste, let thy compassions meet us;
For we are brought very low.
9 Help us, O God of our salvation,
On account of the honor of thy name;
And rescue us, and cover over our sins,
For the sake of thy name.
10 Wherefore should the heathen say: Where is their God?
Let there be known among the heathen, in our sight,
The avenging of the blood of thy servants that is shed.
11 Let the sighing of the prisoner come before thee;
According to the greatness of thine arm spare those appointed to death.
12 And return to our neighbors sevenfold into their bosom,
Their reproach, wherewith they reproached thee, O Lord.
13 And we, thy people, and flock of thy pasture,
Will give thanks to thee forever;
To generation and generation we will recount thy praise.

V. 3. There is none to bury.] To do the office of burying.

V. 5, 2d member. Will thy jealousy burn like fire?] Jealousy, of every rival in the regard of his people. Compare the remark on Ps. 73 : 27; and for the whole expression, see Deut. 32 : 21, 22.

V. 8. Meet us.] Anticipate our need.

V. 11, 2d member. The greatness of thine arm.] Its power to reach d rescue those who are in greatest need.

PSALM LXXX.

To the chief Musician. To [the melody] "Lilies, a Testimony." A Psalm of Asaph.

1 SHEPHERD of Israel give ear;
Thou that leadest Joseph as a flock,
Thou that sittest above the cherubim, shine forth.
2 Before Ephraim, and Benjamin, and Manasseh,
Rouse up thy might,
And come for our salvation.
3 O God, restore us;
And cause thy face to shine, and we shall be saved.
4 Jehovah, God of hosts,
How long art thou angry at the prayer of thy people?
5 Thou hast made them eat the bread of tears,
And given them tears to drink by the measure.
6 Thou makest us a strife to our neighbors;
And our enemies make themselves sport.
7 O God of hosts, restore us;
And cause thy face to shine, and we shall be saved.
8 A vine thou didst remove out of Egypt,
Didst drive out nations, and plant it.
9 Thou hast cleared away before it;
And it struck down its roots, and it filled the land.
10 The mountains were covered with its shade,
And its boughs were as the cedars of God.
11 And it sent out its branches unto the sea,
And its suckers to the river.
12 Wherefore hast thou broken down its walls,
And all pluck it that pass by the way?

V. 5. By the measure.] By the measure-full, in abundance.

V. 10. Were as the cedars of God.] Not that such a vine ever literally existed; but the figure represents the wonderful growth of the people as literally foretold in Gen. 28 : 14, Josh. 1 : 4, and elsewhere.*

* There is no occasion, therefore, to shrink from the literal rendering of the words, as some have done.

13 The boar out of the wood wastes it,
And the beast of the field feeds on it.
14 O God of hosts, return we pray.
Look from heaven, and behold,
And visit this vine;
15 And shelter what thy right hand planted,
And the child thou hast made strong for thyself.
16 It is burned with fire; it is cut down;
At the rebuke of thy countenance they perish.
17 Let thy hand be over the man of thy right hand,
Over the son of man whom thou madest strong for thyself.
18 And we will not go back;
Thou wilt quicken us, and we will call on thy name.
19 Jehovah, God of hosts, restore us;
Cause thy face to shine, and we shall be saved.

PSALM LXXXI.

To the chief Musician. On the Gittith. [A Psalm] of Asaph.

1 Make a joyful noise to God, our strength;
Shout aloud to the God of Jacob.
2 Raise a song, and let the timbrel sound,
The sweet harp, with the lute.
3 Blow the trumpet in the new moon;
In the full moon, on the day of our solemn feast.
4 For this is a statute for Israel,
An ordinance of the God of Jacob.
5 He appointed it for a testimony in Joseph,
When he went forth over the land of Egypt.
I heard a language that I knew not.

V. 15. Made strong.] Reared to a condition of maturity and strength.

Psalm lxxxi. (title). On the Gittith.] See the remark on Ps. viii. (title).

V. 5. Went forth over the land of Egypt.] See Ex. 11 : 4, "At midnight will I go forth in the midst of Egypt;" and compare Mic. 1 : 3.

V. 5, 3d member. Language that I knew not.] Either the language of Egypt, a foreign tongue to the Hebrews; or, as now generally under-

6 I removed his shoulder from the burden,
His hands withdrew from the basket.
7 In the distress thou didst call, and I rescued thee ;
I answered thee in the veil of thunder.
I proved thee at the Waters of Strife. (*Pause.*)
8 Hear, O my people, and I will testify against thee,
O Israel, if thou wilt hearken to me.
9 There shall not be in thee a strange god,
And thou shalt not worship a foreign god.
10 I, Jehovah, am thy God,
He that brought thee up out of the land of Egypt.
Open thy mouth wide, and I will fill it.
11 And my people hearkened not to my voice,
And Israel did not incline to me.
12 And I gave them up to the stubbornness of their heart;
They go on in their own counsels.
13 If my people hearkened to my voice,
If Israel would walk in my ways ;
14 Soon would I humble their enemies,
And again lay my hand on their foes.
15 Haters of Jehovah should profess submission to him ;
And their time should be forever.
16 He would feed them with the marrow of the wheat ;
And with honey out of the rock would I satisfy thee.

---

stood, the encouraging language of their Deliverer (see the two following verses), to them new and unintelligible. Compare Ex. 6 : 9, "They hearkened not to Moses, for anguish of spirit, and for cruel bondage."

V. 6. The basket.] For carrying burdens, with the hands or on the head, as represented on the monuments of ancient Egypt. Compare Gen. 40 : 16, 17, and the writer's note on the passage.*

V. 7. Veil of thunder.] The thunder-cloud.

V. 10, 3d member. The implication is, that no other source of good need be sought.

V. 15. Their time.] Israel's time ; his duration as a favored people.

V. 16. The marrow of the wheat.] The most nutritious wheat.

* The word may also be translated pots ; namely, earthen pots, the making of which was doubtless a part of the labor of the Hebrews "in clay" (not "mortar," Ex. 1 : 14), during their bondage in Egypt. But this meaning of the word is less pertinent than the other, in the connection here.

PSALM LXXXII.

A Psalm of Asaph.

God stands in the congregation of the Mighty One;
In the midst of the gods he judges.
2 How long will ye judge wrongfully,
And accept the persons of the wicked? (*Pause.*)
3 Judge the weak and the orphan;
Do justice to the afflicted and poor.
4 Deliver the weak and needy;
Rescue from the hand of the wicked.
5 They know not, and they will not understand;
They go their way in darkness.
All the foundations of the earth are shaken.
6 I, I have said: Ye are gods,
And sons of the Highest, all of you.
7 Yet surely as men shall ye die,
And as any of the princes shall ye fall.
8 Arise, O God, judge the earth;
For thou shalt inherit among all the nations.

PSALM LXXXIII.

A Song. A Psalm of Asaph.

1 O God, do not thou be quiet;
Do not hold thy peace, and do not rest, O Mighty One.
2 For lo, thine enemies rage,
And thy haters have lifted up the head.

V. 1, 2d member. Gods.] So magistrates, as representing God's judicial sovereignty (Rom. 13 : 4), are called in Ex. 21 : 6, 22 : 8, 9 (properly gods, instead of judges.)

V. 5, 3d member. Foundations.] Of social order; those institutions of civil government on which the peace and security of society rest. When these fail, society is disorganized, and falls into ruin. Compare Ps. 11 : 3, and Ps. 75 : 3.

V. 8. Shalt inherit among.] Shall have inheritance among them.

3 Against thy people they take crafty counsel,
And they consult together against thy hidden ones.
4 They have said : Come, let us destroy them from being a nation,
And let the name of Israel be remembered no more.
5 For they have taken counsel in heart together.
Against thee they make a league ;
6 The tents of Edom and the Ishmaelites,
Moab and the Hagarites ;
7 Gebal and Ammon and Amalek,
Philistia, with the inhabitants of Tyre.
8 Also Asshur is joined with them ;
They have become an arm to the sons of Lot. (*Pause.*)
9 Do to them as to Midian,
As to Sisera, as to Jabin, at the brook Kishon.
10 They were destroyed at Endor ;
They became dung for the ground.
11 Make them, their nobles, as Oreb and as Zeeb,
And all their princes as Zebah and as Zalmunna.
12 Who have said : Let us take possession for ourselves,
Of the dwelling-places of God.
13 My God, make them like the whirling dust,
Like chaff before the wind.
14 As fire consumes a forest,
And as a flame kindles mountains ;
15 So wilt thou pursue them with thy tempest,
And with thy whirlwind terrify them.
16 Fill their face with shame,
And they shall seek thy name, Jehovah!
17 They shall be shamed and terror-stricken forever,
And shall be confounded and perish.
18 And they shall know that thou, thy name Jehovah, alone,
Art Most High over all the earth.

V. 3. Thy hidden ones.] Those under thy protection. Compare Pss. 17 : 8 ; 27 : 5 ; 31 : 20 ; 64 : 2 ; 91 : 1.

V. 5. In heart.] The source of their evil machinations. Compare Ps. 58 : 2.

PSALM LXXXIV.

To the chief Musician. On the Gittith. A Psalm of the Sons of Korah.

1 How lovely are thy dwellings,
O Jehovah of hosts!
2 My soul longs, yea even faints,
For the courts of Jehovah.
My heart and my flesh cry out for the living God.
3 Yea, the sparrow has found a house,
And the swallow has a nest,
Where she lays her young,—
Thine altars, Jehovah of hosts,
My king, and my God!
4 Happy they who dwell in thy house;
Continually do they praise thee. (*Pause.*)
5 Happy the man who has his strength in thee,
In their heart the pilgrim-ways.
6 Passing through the valley of weeping,
They make it a place of fountains;
Yea, the autumn rain clothes it with blessings.
7 They go from strength to strength;
They appear, each one, before God in Zion.
8 Jehovah, God of hosts, hear my prayer;
Give ear, O God of Jacob. (*Pause.*)
9 Behold, O God, our shield,
And look on the face of thine anointed.
10 For a day in thy courts is better than a thousand;
I would rather be a doorkeeper in the house of my God,
Than dwell in the tents of wickedness.
11 For Jehovah God is a sun and a shield;
Grace and glory will Jehovah give.
He withholds no good from them that walk uprightly.
12 Jehovah of hosts,
Happy the man that trusts in thee!

V. 5. The pilgrim-ways.] By which the people went up to the annual feasts. Compare Ps. 122 : 4.

PSALM LXXXV.

To the chief Musician. A Psalm of the Sons of Korah.

1 Thou wast favorable, O Jehovah, to thy land ;
Thou didst turn the captivity of Jacob.
2 Thou didst take away the iniquity of thy people,
Didst cover all their sin. (*Pause.*)
3 Thou didst withdraw all thy wrath ;
Didst turn away from the burning of thine anger.
4 Restore us, O God of our salvation,
And cause thy displeasure against us to cease.
5 Wilt thou forever be angry with us ?
Wilt thou draw out thine anger to generation and generation ?
6 Wilt not thou again revive us,
And thy people shall rejoice in thee ?
7 Let us see thy mercy, O Jehovah,
And grant us thy salvation.
8 I will hear what the Mighty One, Jehovah, will speak ;
For he will speak peace to his people and to his saints :
And let them not turn again to folly.
9 Surely, his salvation is near to them that fear him,
That glory may dwell in our land.
10 Mercy and truth have met together ;
Righteousness and peace have kissed each other.
11 Truth springs up out of the earth,
And righteousness looks down from heaven.

VV. 1–3. Wast, etc.] In former seasons of national calamity.

V. 1. Turn the captivity.] Compare Ps. 14 : 7, and the writer's remark on Job 42 : 10.*

V. 4. Restore us.] *Or*, Turn to us.

V. 12. The [promised] good.] See Lev. 26 : 4, from which the words of the next line are taken.

* " Captivity was then no unusual calamity ; and the phrase naturally became a proverbial one, for restoration from deep affliction to former prosperity." (*Book of Job, Part Second*, p. 85.) The phrase may be used here in its literal sense ; but not necessarily, as these examples show.

12 Yea, Jehovah will give the [promised] good,
And our land will yield its increase.
13 Righteousness shall go before him,
And shall make his footsteps a way.

PSALM LXXXVI.

A Prayer of David.

1 INCLINE thine ear, O Jehovah, and answer me,
For I am poor and needy.
2 Preserve my soul, for I am a beloved one.
Save thy servant, O thou my God,
That trusts in thee.
3 Be gracious to me, O Lord,
For to thee do I cry all the day.
4 Rejoice the soul of thy servant;
For to thee do I lift up my soul.
5 For thou, Lord, art good and ready to forgive,
And abundant in mercy to all that call upon thee.
6 Give ear, O Jehovah, to my prayer,
And attend to the voice of my supplications.
7 In the day of my distress I call upon thee ;
For thou wilt answer me.
8 There is none like thee among the gods, O Lord,
And no works like thine.
9 All nations, which thou hast made,
Shall come and bow down before thee, O Lord,
And shall give glory to thy name.
10 For thou art great, and doest wonders ;
Thou art God alone.
11 Teach me, Jehovah, thy way ;
I will walk in thy truth.
Unite my heart to fear thy name.

V. 13 Shall make his footsteps a way.] The righteousness, that precedes and directs his steps, shall make them a way for his people to follow him.

12 I will praise thee, O Lord my God, with my whole heart,
And will glorify thy name forevermore.
13 For great is thy mercy toward me;
And thou hast rescued my soul from the underworld beneath.
14 O God, the proud have risen up against me,
And an assembly of the violent have sought after my soul,
And have not set thee before them.
15 But thou, O Lord, art a God compassionate and gracious,
Long-suffering, and abundant in goodness and truth.
16 Turn toward me, and be gracious to me;
Give thy strength to thy servant,
And grant deliverance to the son of thy handmaid.
17 Show me a token for good;
And they that hate me shall see and be ashamed,
Because thou, Jehovah, hast helped me, and comforted me.

PSALM LXXXVII.

A Psalm of the Sons of Korah. A Song.

1 His foundation is in the holy mountains.
2 Jehovah loves the gates of Zion,
More than all the dwellings of Jacob.
3 Glorious things are spoken of thee,
O city of God. (*Pause.*)
4 I will make mention of Rahab, and Babylon, among them
that know me;
Behold, Philistia, and Tyre, with Ethiopia;
This one was born there.
5 And of Zion it shall be said:
This and that man was born in her;
And He, the Most High, will establish her.

V. 3. Glorious things are spoken of thee.] With this and the following three verses compare such prophetic views as Is. 2 : 2, 3, 11 : 10, and their fulfilment, Eph. 2 : 11–20, Coloss. 3 : 11. Zion is to become a new birthplace, to all the nations.

V. 4, 3d member. There.] The "city of God" (v. 3) is meant.

6 Jehovah will count, in writing up the peoples,
This one was born there. (*Pause.*)
7 And singers as well as players [say :]
All my springs are in thee.

PSALM LXXXVIII.

A Song. A Psalm of the Sons of Korah. To the chief Musician. On occasion of affliction by sickness. Didactic [Psalm] of Heman the Ezrahite.

1 JEHOVAH, God of my salvation,
By day I cry out, by night, before thee.
2 Let my prayer come before thee ;
Incline thine ear to my cry.
3 For my soul is full of troubles ;
And my life draws near to the underworld.
4 I am reckoned with them that go down to the pit ;
I am become as a man without strength ;
5 Forsaken among the dead,
Like the slain that lie in the grave ;
Whom thou rememberest no more,
And they are cut off from thy hand.
6 Thou hast laid me in the lowest pit ;
In dark places, in the depths.
7 Thy wrath lies heavy on me,
And with all thy waves thou hast afflicted me. (*Pause.*)
8 Thou hast put my acquaintance far away from me ;
Thou hast made me an abomination to them ;
Shut up, and I can not go forth.
9 My eye wastes away through affliction.
I call upon thee, Jehovah, all the day ;
I spread out my hands unto thee.

V. 6. In writing up the peoples.] In registering, or enrolling them. Compare Is. 4 : 3 ; properly, every one that is inscribed unto life (in the book of life).

V. 5. Cut off from thy hand.] Removed beyond its reach.

10 Wilt thou do wonders to the dead?
Or will the shades rise up and praise thee? (*Pause.*)
11 Will thy loving-kindness be told in the grave,
Thy faithfulness in destruction?
12 Will thy wonders be made known in the darkness,
And thy righteousness in the land of forgetfulness?
13 And I unto thee, Jehovah, have cried for help;
And in the morning my prayer shall come before thee.
14 Wherefore, O Jehovah, dost thou cast off my soul,
Dost hide thy face from me?
15 I am afflicted, and ready to expire, from my youth;
I have borne thy terrors; am in despair.
16 Thine indignations have passed over me,
Thy terrors have consumed me.
17 They have encompassed me like waters all the day;
Together they beset me round.
18 Thou hast put far from me lover and friend;—
My acquaintance—the place of darkness!

V. 10. The shades.] Disembodied spirits, that survive the death of the body, and exist separate from it. See the writer's note on Job (*Book of Job, Part Second*), ch. 26 : 5.

This often repeated recognition, in the language itself, of the continued separate existence of the soul, after the dissolution of the body, is lost to the reader of the common English version.

V. 18. The sentiment is: My former associates are estranged (compare v 8, "thou hast made me an abomination to them"); and for my acquaintance now, I have only darkness in its gloomy abode!

The whole tenor of the psalm, and the express declaration in v. 8, show that the common idea, of the removal of "lover, friend, and acquaintance" by death (founded on the mistranslation of the verse in our common English version) is not the one intended by the Psalmist. However dear the thought thus originated may have become to the Christian mind, it must give place to the true meaning of the sacred writer.*

* Some may be interested to know, that it was not the original rendering of our Bible. The oldest rendering of the English Bible from the Hebrew is: "My lovers and friends hast thou put away from me, and turned away my acquaintance;" (the same sentiment as in v. 8). So the English Bible of 1535, and of 1537. To the same effect is the Genevan Version (1560): "My lovers and friends hast thou put away from me, [*and*] mine acquaintance hid themselves." Cranmer's erroneous construction and rendering of the last clause, "and hid mine acquaintance out of my sight," was followed in the Bishops' Bible (1568), "Thou hast put away far from me my friend and neighbor, (*thou hast hid*) mine acquaintance out of sight" (margin, "in darkness"), and thus led the way to the false construction and sentiment in King James's version.

PSALM LXXXIX.

Didactic [Psalm] of Ethan the Ezrahite.

1 I WILL sing of the mercies of Jehovah forever;
To generation and generation will I make known thy faithfulness with my mouth.
2 I said: Mercy shall be built up forever;
The heavens—in them thou wilt establish thy faithfulness.
3 I have made a covenant for my chosen one,
I have sworn to David my servant:
4 Forever will I establish thy seed,
And build up thy throne to generation and generation. (*Pause.*)
5 And the heavens praise thy wonders, O Jehovah,
Yea, thy faithfulness in the assembly of the holy ones.
6 For who in the skies can be compared to Jehovah,
Is like to Jehovah among the sons of the mighty;
7 A God greatly to be feared in the council of the holy ones,
And terrible above all that are round about him?
8 Jehovah, God of hosts,
Who is mighty like thee, O Jah,
And thy faithfulness is round about thee.
9 Thou rulest the swelling of the sea;
When its billows rise, thou stillest them.
10 Thou, thou didst crush Rahab like the slain;
With thy strong arm thou didst scatter thy enemies.
11 The heavens are thine; thine also is the earth;
The world and its fullness, thou didst found them.

V. 2. In them.] So as to be as enduring and unchanging as they.

V. 3. For my chosen one.] In his behalf. Not with him, as one of two parties to the covenant. Compare the writer's remark on Gen. 15 : 9–17.

V. 6. In the skies.] Compare the expression in Eph. 2 : 2.

V. 6, 2d member. The mighty.] Compare the remark on Ps. 78 : 25.

V. 8. Is round about thee.] A perpetual presence, attending the Divine in all its manifestations.

12 North and South, thou didst create them ;
Tabor and Hermon triumph in thy name.
13 Thine is an arm with might ;
Strong is thy hand, high is thy right hand.
14 Righteousness and judgment are the foundation of thy throne ;
Mercy and truth wait before thee.
15 Happy the people that know the joyful sound ;
Jehovah, in the light of thy countenance shall they walk.
16 In thy name do they exult all the day,
And in thy righteousness are they exalted.
17 For thou art the glory of their strength ;
And in thy favor our horn is exalted.
18 For to Jehovah belongs our shield,
And to the Holy One of Israel, our king.
19 Then thou didst speak in vision to thy beloved one,
And saidst : I have laid help on a mighty one,
Have exalted one chosen out of the people.
20 I have found David, my servant ;
With my holy oil have I anointed him.
21 With whom my hand shall be established ;
Also my arm shall strengthen him.
22 No enemy shall exact of him,
Or son of wickedness oppress him.
23 And I will beat down his foes before him,
And will smite them that hate him.
24 And my faithfulness and my mercy shall be with him,
And in my name shall his horn be exalted.
25 And I set his hand on the sea,
And his right hand on the rivers.
26 He will cry unto me : Thou art my father ;
My God, and the rock of my salvation.
27 I too will make him the firstborn,
Highest of the kings of the earth.

V. 12. Tabor and Hermon.] Representing the East and West of the land.

V. 14. Wait before thee.] For thy commands.

28 My mercy will I keep for him forever,
And my covenant is sure to him.
29 And I establish his seed forever,
And his throne as the days of heaven.
30 If his sons shall forsake my law,
And walk not in my judgments;
31 If they shall profane my statutes,
And keep not my commandments;
32 Then will I visit their transgressions with a rod,
And their iniquity with stripes.
33 But my loving-kindness will I not withdraw from him,
And will not be false to my faith.
34 I will not profane my covenant,
Nor alter what has gone forth from my lips.
35 Once have I sworn by my holiness;
I will not lie to David.
36 His seed shall be forever,
And his throne as the sun before me.
37 As the moon shall it stand fast forever,
And as the witness in the skies is sure. (*Pause.*)
38 But thou, thou hast cast off and abhorred;
Thou hast been wroth with thine anointed.
39 Thou hast made void the covenant of thy servant;
Thou hast profaned to the earth his crown.
40 Thou hast broken down all his walls;
Hast made his defenses a ruin.
41 They plunder him, all that pass by the way;
He has become the scorn of his neighbors.
42 Thou hast exalted the right hand of his foes;
Hast made all his enemies rejoice.
43 Yea, thou turnest back the edge of his sword,
And hast not made him stand in the battle.
44 Thou hast made his brightness to cease;
And his throne thou hast cast down to the earth.

V. 37. "The witness in the skies" most naturally suggests the "covenant-sign," the witness to the "perpetual covenant between God and every living being." Gen. 9 : 12–17 (revised version).

45 Thou hast cut short the days of his youth;
Thou hast covered over him with shame. (*Pause.*)
46 How long, O Jehovah! Wilt thou hide thyself forever?
Shall thy wrath burn like fire?
47 Remember what is my fleeting life;
Why hast thou for naught created all the sons of men?
48 What man shall live, and not see death,
Shall deliver his soul from the grasp of the underworld? (*Pause.*)
49 Where are thy former mercies, O Lord,
Which thou didst swear to David in thy faithfulness?
50 Remember, Lord, the reproach of thy servants,
That I bear in my bosom of all the many peoples;
51 Wherewith thine enemies have reproached, O Jehovah,
Wherewith they have reproached the footsteps of thine anointed.

BLESSED BE JEHOVAH FOREVERMORE.

AMEN AND AMEN.

FOURTH BOOK.

PSALM XC.

A Prayer of Moses, the Man of God.

1 Lord, thou hast been our dwelling-place in all generations.
2 Before the mountains were brought forth,
And thou gavest birth to the earth and the world,
Even from everlasting to everlasting thou art God.
3 Thou turnest man to dust;
And sayest: Return, ye sons of men.
4 For a thousand years, in thy sight,
Are as yesterday when it passes away,
And a watch in the night.
5 Thou sweepest them away, they are a sleep;
In the morning as the grass that springs up;
6 In the morning it flourishes and springs up,
At evening, it is cut down and withers.
7 For we consume away in thine anger,
And in thy wrath are we troubled.
8 Thou hast set our iniquities before thee,
Our hidden things in the light of thy countenance.

VV. 5, 6. An image of fleeting human life. It passes away in the death-slumber; succeeded by new life, as the grass that springs up freshly in the dew of the morning, to wither in its turn, and die. The comparison in v. 5, 2d member, is abruptly and not fully expressed, but the thought is clearly indicated.*

* Fully expressed, the thought would be: They pass away in the night-slumber of the grave; followed by the morning life of another generation, as the morning grass springs up in place of that which has withered and died.

9 For all our days pass away in thy wrath;
We spend our years like a thought.
10 The days of our years,—in them are threescore years and ten;
And if, through strength, fourscore years,
Yet is their pride toil and vanity;
For it is soon past, and we fly away.
11 Who knows the power of thine anger,
And as the fear of thee, thy wrath?
12 So teach to number our days,
That we may get a heart of wisdom.
13 Return O Jehovah; how long!
And have pity on thy servants.
14 Satisfy us with thy mercy in the morning,
That we may rejoice and be glad, all our days.
15 Make us glad according to the days thou hast afflicted us,
The years we have seen evil.
16 Let thy work appear unto thy servants,
And thy majesty upon their sons.
17 And let the beauty of Jehovah our God be upon us;
And the work of our hands establish thou upon us,
Yea, the work of our hands, establish thou it.

V. 9, 2d member. Our years like a thought.] With the rapidity and suddenness of thought, they are gone.

V. 10, 1st member. In them.] The emphatic form of the original, which should not be suppressed.

V. 10, 3d member. Their pride.] Their vain boast.—Toil and vanity.] Anxious labor, with no result.

V. 11. As the fear of thee.] In proportion to, and in accordance with it. As the fear of God requires, and as is due to it.

V. 14. In the morning.] The morning of deliverance and triumph, after this night of humiliation. Compare Ps. 46 : 5. The sentiment is: Let morning return, and with it thy satisfying mercy. "Morning denotes that there has hitherto been night in Israel, and the dawn of an era of grace." *(Delitzsch.)*

V. 17, 2d member. Establish thou upon us.] By an influence from above, as descending upon us.

PSALM XCI.

1 Dwelling in the covert of the Most High,
He abides in the shadow of the Almighty.
2 I will say of Jehovah: My refuge and my fortress;
My God, I will trust in him.
3 For he, he will rescue thee from the snare of the fowler,
From the destroying pestilence.
4 With his feathers he will cover thee,
And under his wings shalt thou trust;
His truth, a shield and buckler!
5 Thou shalt not be afraid of the terror by night,
Of the arrow that flies by day;
6 Of the pestilence that walks in darkness,
Of the contagion that wastes at noon-day.
7 A thousand shall fall at thy side,
And ten thousand at thy right hand;
To thee it shall not come nigh.
8 Only with thine eyes shalt thou look on,
And see the reward of the wicked.
9 Because thou hast made Jehovah,--my refuge,
The Most High, thy dwelling-place;
10 There shall no evil befall thee,
And no plague shall come nigh thy tent.
11 For he will give his angels charge concerning thee,
To keep thee in all thy ways.
12 On their hands shall they bear thee up,
Lest thou dash thy foot against a stone.
13 Thou shalt tread on the lion and the adder;
The young lion and dragon shalt thou trample under foot.
14 For he has set his love upon me, and I will deliver him;
I will set him on high, because he knows my name.

V. 9. Thy dwelling-place.] See v. 1.

V. 10, 2d member. Tent.] Dwelling is meant; but in allusion to its simplest and primitive form.

15 He will call upon me, and I will answer him;
I will be with him in trouble;
I will rescue him, and will honor him.
16 With length of days will I satisfy him,
And will cause him to see my salvation.

PSALM XCII.

A Psalm. A Song for the Sabbath Day.

1 It is good to give thanks to Jehovah,
And to sing praise to thy name, O Most High;
2 To declare thy loving-kindness in the morning,
And thy faithfulness every night;
3 To a ten-stringed instrument, and to the lute,
To the murmuring sound on the harp.
4 For thou hast gladdened me, Jehovah, by thy work;
In the works of thy hands I will triumph.
5 How great are thy works, O Jehovah!
Thy counsels are very deep.
6 A brutish man knows not,
Nor does a fool understand this.
7 When the wicked spring up as grass,
And all the workers of iniquity flourish;
It is that they may be destroyed forever.
8 And thou, Jehovah, art on high forevermore.
9 For lo, thine enemies, Jehovah,
For lo, thine enemies shall perish;
All the workers of iniquity shall be scattered.
10 But my horn thou wilt exalt as of the wild-ox;
I am anointed with fresh oil.
11 And my eye had its desire on them that lie in wait for me,
And my ear on evil-doers that rise up against me.

V. 8. On high.] Supreme over all.

V. 10. The wild-ox.] For the natural traits of this powerful and untamed animal, see Job 39 : 9-12 (revised version.)

12 The righteous shall flourish like the palm-tree,
Shall grow like a cedar in Lebanon.
13 Planted in the house of Jehovah,
They shall flourish in the courts of our God.
14 Still shall they bear fruit in hoary age;
Full of sap, and green shall they be.
15 To show that Jehovah is upright;
My rock, and no unrighteousness is in him.

PSALM XCIII.

1 JEHOVAH reigns; he is clothed with majesty.
Jehovah is clothed with strength; he has girded himself.
Yea, the world shall stand fast, it shall not be moved.
2 Thy throne stands fast from of old;
Thou art from everlasting.
3 The floods have lifted up, O Jehovah,
The floods have lifted up their voice;
The floods lift up their dashing waves.
4 Mightier is Jehovah on high,
Than the voice of many waters,
The mighty waves of the sea.
5 Thy testimonies are very sure.
Holiness becomes thy house,
O Jehovah, forever.

PSALM XCIV.

1 GOD of vengeance, Jehovah,
God of vengeance, shine forth.
2 Lift up thyself, thou judge of the earth;
Return a recompense upon the proud.
3 How long shall the wicked, O Jehovah,
How long shall the wicked triumph?
4 They belch out, they speak rudely,
They boast themselves, all the workers of iniquity.

5 They grind thy people, O Jehovah,
And thy heritage they oppress.
6 The widow and the stranger they kill,
And orphans they murder.
7 And they say: Jah will not see,
And the God of Jacob will not attend.
8 Understand, ye brutish among the people;
And ye fools, when will ye be wise?
9 He that planted the ear, shall he not hear?
Or he that formed the eye, shall not he behold?
10 He that chastises nations, shall not he correct,
He that teaches man knowledge?
11 Jehovah knows the thoughts of man,
That they are vanity.
12 Happy the man whom thou chastenest, O Jah,
And teachest him out of thy law;
13 To give him rest from the days of evil,
Until a pit shall be dug for the wicked.
14 For Jehovah will not cast off his people,
And his inheritance he will not forsake.
15 For unto righteousness shall judgment return,
And after it, all the upright in heart.
16 Who will rise up for me against evil-doers;
Who will take his stand for me against workers of iniquity?
17 Unless Jehovah were my help,
Soon would my soul dwell in silence.
18 When I say: My feet waver,—
Thy mercy holds me up.
19 In the multitude of my thoughts within me,
Thy comforts soothe my spirit.
20 Shall the throne of iniquity be allied to thee,
Framing mischief against law?
21 They gather in crowds against the soul of the righteous,
And condemn innocent blood.

V. 15. Judgment (the judicial act, the administration of law) shall return to righteousness (the eternal principles of right).

V. 17. In silence.] The silence of the grave.

22 But Jehovah has been a high tower for me,
And my God a rock of refuge.
23 And he returned upon them their iniquity,
And cut them off in their wickedness.
Jehovah, our God, will cut them off!

PSALM XCV.

1 Come, let us sing aloud to Jehovah,
Let us shout to the rock of our salvation.
2 Let us come before his face with thanksgiving,
And shout to him in songs.
3 For Jehovah is a great God,
And a great king above all gods;
4 In whose hand are the recesses of the earth,
And the treasures of the mountains are his;
5 Whose is the sea, and he made it,
And his hands formed the dry land.
6 Come, let us worship and bow down;
Let us kneel before Jehovah our maker.
7 For he is our God,
And we are the people of his pasture, and flock of his hand.
8 To-day, if ye will hearken to his voice!
Harden not your heart, as at Meribah,
As in the day of Massah, in the wilderness.
9 Where your fathers tempted me,
They tried me, also saw my work.
10 Forty years did I loathe the generation;
And I said: They are a people that err in heart,
And they know not my ways;
11 Wherefore, I have sworn in my wrath,
They shall not enter into my rest.

V. 23. 3d member. Will cut them off.] Will continue to do it.

V. 4. Recesses of the earth.] Containing its hidden wealth.

V. 8. If ye will hearken.] The reward of such obedience is implied, by a common figure of speech. Compare the remark on Ps. 27 : 13.

V. 8. Meribah—Massah.] Ex. 17 : 7 ; Num. 20 : 13 ; Deut. 33 : 8.

V. 11. Num. 14 : 23, 28–30.

PSALM XCVI.

1 Sing to Jehovah a new song;
Sing to Jehovah, all the earth.
2 Sing to Jehovah, bless his name;
Proclaim his salvation from day to day.
3 Declare his glory among the heathen,
His wonders among all the peoples.
4 For great is Jehovah, and greatly to be praised;
He is to be feared above all gods.
5 For all the gods of the peoples are nothings;
And Jehovah made the heavens.
6 Honor and majesty are before him,
Strength and beauty in his holy place.
7 Give to Jehovah, ye families of peoples,
Give to Jehovah glory and strength.
8 Give to Jehovah the glory of his name;
Bring an offering, and come in to his courts.
9 Worship Jehovah in the beauty of holiness;
Tremble before him, all the earth.
10 Say among the heathen, Jehovah reigns;
Yea, the world shall stand fast, it shall not be moved;
He will judge the peoples in rectitude.
11 Let the heavens rejoice, and the earth exult;
Let the sea roar, and the fullness thereof;
12 Let the field triumph, and all that is therein;
Then shall all the trees of the wood be joyful;

V. 5. Nothings.] In Isaiah, a favorite designation of idols (compare 1 Cor. 8 : 4). Here, as in 1 Chron. 16 : 26, the connection requires the literal translation of the word.

Compare the sarcastic and striking characterization of these "nothings," in which the heathen trusted, in Is. 44 : 12–17.

V. 7. Families of peoples.] Each of the peoples being one great family, descended from a common parent. See the writer's note on Gen. 12 : 3, and compare "families of nations," in Ps. 22 : 27.

V. 10. The world shall stand fast.] An image of stability and security in all civil and social relations, as a consequence of Jehovah's righteous sway. Compare the opposite image in Ps. 75 : 3.

13 Before Jehovah; for he comes,
For he comes to judge the earth.
14 He will judge the world in righteousness,
And the peoples in his faithfulness.

PSALM XCVII.

1 JEHOVAH reigns, let the earth exult;
Let the multitude of isles be glad.
2 Clouds and darkness are round about him;
Righteousness and judgment are the foundation of his throne.
3 Fire goes before him,
And burns up his foes on every side.
4 His lightnings lightened the world;
The earth saw, and quaked.
5 Mountains melted like wax at the presence of Jehovah,
At the presence of the Lord of the whole earth.
6 The heavens declared his righteousness,
And all the peoples saw his glory.
7 Ashamed shall all be that serve a graven image,
That make their boast of idols.
Worship him, all ye gods.
8 Zion heard, and was glad,
And the daughters of Judah exulted,
Because of thy judgments, O Jehovah.
9 For thou, Jehovah, art Most High over all the earth,
Art greatly exalted above all gods.
10 Ye that love Jehovah, hate evil;
He preserves the souls of his saints;
He rescues them out of the hand of the wicked.
11 Light is sown for the righteous,
And gladness for the upright in heart.
12 Be glad, ye righteous, in Jehovah,
And give thanks to his holy memorial.

V. 12. His holy memorial.] His sacred memorial name, JEHOVAH. See the remark on Ps. 30 : 4.

PSALM XCVIII.

A Psalm.

1 Sing to Jehovah a new song;
For he has done wondrous things.
His right hand, and his holy arm, have wrought salvation for him.
2 Jehovah has made known his salvation;
Before the eyes of the heathen has he revealed his righteousness.
3 He has remembered his loving-kindness and his truth,
Toward the house of Israel.
All the ends of the earth have seen
The salvation of our God.
4 Shout to Jehovah, all the earth;
Break forth, and be joyful, and sing praise.
5 Sing praise to Jehovah with the harp,
With the harp, and the voice of song.
6 With cornets, and sound of trumpet,
Shout before the king, Jehovah.
7 Let the sea roar, and the fullness thereof,
The world, and they that dwell therein;
8 Let the floods clap their hands,
Let the mountains be joyful together;
9 Before Jehovah; for he comes to judge the earth.
He will judge the world in righteousness,
And the peoples in rectitude.

PSALM XCIX.

1 Jehovah reigns, let the people tremble;
He sits above the cherubim, let the earth shake.
2 Jehovah is great in Zion;
And high is he above all the peoples.
3 Let them praise thy great and terrible name;
It is holy!

4 And the king's strength loves judgment;
Thou dost establish equity;
Thou dost execute judgment and righteousness in Jacob.
5 Exalt ye Jehovah, our God,
And worship at his footstool.
He is holy!
6 Moses and Aaron among his priests,
And Samuel among them that call on his name,—
They called upon Jehovah, and he answered them.
7 In the pillar of cloud he spoke to them.
They kept his testimonies, and the statutes he gave them.
8 Jehovah, our God, thou didst answer them;
A forgiving God wast thou to them,
And one that took vengeance on their deeds.
9 Exalt Jehovah, our God,
And worship at his holy mount.
For Jehovah, our God, is holy.

PSALM C.

A Psalm of Thanksgiving.

1 Shout to Jehovah, all the earth.
2 Serve Jehovah with gladness;
Come before him with exultation.
3 Know that Jehovah, he is God;
He it is that made us, and we are his,
His people, and the flock of his pasture.
4 Enter into his gates with thanksgiving,
His courts with praise;
Give thanks to him, bless his name.
5 For Jehovah is good; his mercy is forever,
And his faithfulness to generation and generation.

V. 8, 2d and 3d members. Both attributes were conspicuously shown, in God's dealings with his people. The latter are included in the pronouns *(them, their)*, the intercession having been made on their behalf.

PSALM CI.

A Psalm of David.

1 Of mercy and of judgment will I sing;
To thee, Jehovah, will I sing praise.
2 I will act wisely in a perfect way.
When wilt thou come to me!
I will walk in the integrity of my heart within my house.
3 I will set no wicked thing before my eyes.
The work of them that turn aside I hate;
It shall not cleave to me.
4 A froward heart shall depart from me;
An evil man I will not know.
5 He that secretly slanders his neighbor,
Him will I cut off.
He that is of a high look and a proud heart,
Him will I not bear.
6 My eyes are on the faithful of the land,
That they may dwell with me.
He that walks in a perfect way,
He shall serve me.
7 He that practices deceit shall not dwell within my house;
He that speaks lies shall not abide in my sight.
8 Morning by morning will I destroy all the wicked of the land,
To cut off all workers of iniquity from the city of Jehovah.

PSALM CII.

A prayer of the afflicted, when he is overwhelmed, and pours out his complaint before Jehovah.

1 O Jehovah, hear my prayer,
And let my cry for help come unto thee.
2 Hide not thy face from me in the day when I am in trouble;
Incline to me thine ear;
In the day when I call, make haste to answer me.

3 For my days consume away in smoke,
And my bones glow with heat like a firebrand.
4 My heart is smitten like the grass and dries up;
For I forget to eat my food.
5 Because of the voice of my groaning,
My bones cleave to my flesh.
6 I am like to a pelican of the wilderness;
I have become as an owl among ruins.
7 I watch, and have become
Like a lonely sparrow on the housetop.
8 All the day my enemies reproach me;
They that are mad against me swear by me.
9 For I have eaten ashes like bread,
And have mingled my drink with weeping;
10 Because of thine indignation and thy wrath,
For thou hast taken me up and cast me away.
11 My days are as the lengthened shade;
And I am dried up like the grass.
12 But thou, Jehovah, shalt sit [on the throne] forever,
And thy remembrance is to all generations.
13 Thou wilt arise, wilt have mercy upon Zion;
For it is the time to favor her,
For the set time is come.

V. 3. In smoke.] That vanishes into thin air, leaving no trace. So my days waste unprofitably away.

V. 4. Is smitten like the grass.] As grass is smitten by the scorching heat, and dries up.

V. 6, 2d member. An owl among ruins.] Compare *Smith's Bible Dictionary*, art. Owl, 3.

V. 7. I watch.] Am sleepless.

V. 8. Swear by me.] Compare the form of imprecation. "So let the gods do," as used in 1 Kings 19 : 2, with Is. 65 : 15, Jer. 29 : 22, and the form of blessing in Gen. 48 : 20.*

V. 11. My days (my term of life) are as the lengthened shade,—the lengthening shade of evening, that shows the near approach of night. The comparison, though not strictly expressed, is beautifully suggestive of the thought intended.

* "Swear by me; that is, use me as a formula of execration, imprecating upon others misery like mine." (Dr. Alexander, on the passage.)

14 For thy servants take pleasure in her stones,
And her dust they favor.
15 And the heathen shall fear the name of Jehovah.
And kings of the earth thy glory;
16 Because Jehovah has built up Zion,
Is seen in his glory.
17 He has turned unto the prayer of the destitute,
And has not despised their prayer.
18 This shall be written for the generation to come;
And a people to be created shall praise JAH.
19 Jehovah bent down from his holy height;
Jehovah from heaven looked on the earth;
20 To hear the groaning of the prisoner,
To loose those that are appointed to death;
21 To declare in Zion the name of Jehovah,
And his praise in Jerusalem;
22 When the peoples are gathered together,
And the kingdoms, to serve Jehovah.
23 He has humbled my strength in the way;
He has shortened my days.
24 I say: My God, take me not away in the midst of my days!
Thy years are throughout all generations.
25 Of old thou didst lay the foundation of the earth,
And the heavens are the work of thy hands.
26 They shall perish, but thou shalt endure;
And all of them shall waste away like a garment,
And as a vesture thou wilt change them, and they pass away.
27 But thou art the same,
And thy years shall have no end.
28 The sons of thy servants shall dwell [in the land],
And their seed shall be established before thee.

V. 14. Stones—dust.] Of her ruins. Compare Neh. 4 : 2, 10.

V. 18. Compare, "a people that shall be born," Ps. 22 : 31.

V. 23. In the way.] The way in which his providence is conducting me, in distinction from its certain and glorious issue.

V. 28. Dwell in the land.] The word dwell (in Hebrew) has this special application.

PSALM CIII.

[A Psalm] of David.

1 Bless Jehovah, O my soul,
And all that is within me, [bless] his holy name.
2 Bless Jehovah, O my soul,
And forget not all his benefits.
3 Who forgives all thine iniquities,
Who heals all thy diseases;
4 Who redeems thy life from the pit,
Who crowns thee with loving-kindness and tender mercies;
5 Who satisfies thy mouth with good;
Thy youth renews itself as the eagle.
6 Jehovah executes righteousness,
And judgment, for all the oppressed.
7 He made known his ways to Moses,
His deeds to the sons of Israel.
8 Compassionate and gracious is Jehovah,
Slow to anger, and abundant in mercy.
9 He will not always chide,
Nor keep his anger forever.
10 He has not dealt with us according to our sins,
Nor rewarded us according to our iniquities.
11 For as the heavens are high above the earth,
So great is his mercy toward them that fear him.
12 As far as the east is from the west,
So far has he removed our transgressions from us.
13 As a father has compassion on his children,
Jehovah has compassion on them that fear him.
14 For he knows our frame;
He remembers that we are dust.
15 As for man, his days are as grass;
As the flower of the field, so he flourishes.
16 For the wind passes over it, and it is gone,
And its place shall know it no more.

17 But the mercy of Jehovah is from everlasting, and to everlasting, on them that fear him,
And his righteousness to children's children;
18 To them that keep his covenant,
And to them that remember his precepts to do them.
19 Jehovah has established his throne in the heavens,
And his kingdom rules over all.
20 Bless Jehovah, ye his angels,
The mighty in strength, that execute his word,
Hearkening to the voice of his word.
21 Bless Jehovah, all his hosts,
His ministers, that do his pleasure.
22 Bless Jehovah, all his works,
In all places of his dominion.
Bless Jehovah, O my soul!

PSALM CIV.

1 Bless Jehovah, O my soul!
Jehovah, my God, thou art very great;
Thou art clothed with honor and majesty.
2 Who coverest thyself with light as with a mantle,
Who stretchest out the heavens like a curtain.
3 Who frames his chambers in the waters;
Who makes the clouds his chariot;
Who goes on the wings of the wind.
4 Who makes the winds his messengers,
His ministers,—flaming fire.
5 He founded the earth on its bases,
That it should not be moved forever and ever.
6 Thou didst cover it with the abyss as with a garment;
The waters stood above the mountains.

VV. 6–9. Compare Gen. 1 : 2, and 9, 10. Some suppose the Deluge to be referred to in these verses. But such a reference is not in harmony with the purpose and spirit of this sublime hymn of creation, which celebrates the wonders of the Creator's power in its beneficent exercise.

7 At thy rebuke they fled;
At the voice of thy thunder they hasted away,—
8 While mountains rise, valleys sink,—
To the place which thou didst found for them.
9 A bound thou didst set, that they should not pass over,
Should not return to cover the earth.
10 He sends out springs in the valleys;
They run among the mountains.
11 They give drink to every beast of the field;
The wild asses quench their thirst.
12 Above them dwell the fowls of heaven;
From among the branches they utter a voice.
13 He waters the mountains from his chambers;
The earth is sated with the fruit of thy working.
14 He causes grass to grow for the cattle,
And herbs for the service of man,
Bringing forth food out of the earth.
15 And with wine he gladdens the heart of man;
Making the face to shine with oil;
And with bread he strengthens man's heart.
16 The trees of Jehovah are sated,
Cedars of Lebanon which he planted;
17 Where birds make their nests;
The stork, cypresses are her house.
18 The high mountains are a refuge for wild-goats,
The rocks for the conies.
19 He made the moon for seasons;
The sun knows his going-down.

V. 8. As the waters retire to their place at a lower level, the mountains seem to rise, and the valleys to sink.

V. 9. Compare Job 38 : 10, (Book of Job, revised version):
And appointed it my bound,
And set bars and doors.

V. 13. Is sated.] Receives, in full measure, all that it craves.

V. 16. Sated.] Have, in abundance, all that they crave. Compare v. 13. Vegetable as well as animal life is cared for in the providence of God, and all its wants supplied.

20 Thou dost put darkness, and it is night;
Wherein all the beasts of the forest are in motion.
21 The young lions roar for the prey,
And seek their food from God.
22 The sun arises, they retire,
And couch down in their dens.
23 Man goes forth to his work,
And to his toil, until evening.
24 How manifold are thy works, O Jehovah!
In wisdom hast thou wrought them all.
The earth is full of thy riches.
25 That sea, great and broad on every hand!
Where are moving things, and without number,
Both small and great beasts.
26 There go the ships,
That leviathan thou hast formed to sport therein.
27 They all wait for thee,
To give their food in its season.
28 Thou givest to them, they gather;
Thou openest thy hand, they are sated with good.
29 Thou hidest thy face, they are troubled;
Thou withdrawest their breath, they expire,
And return to their dust.
30 Thou sendest forth thy breath, they are created;
And thou renewest the face of the ground.
31 Let the glory of Jehovah be forever;
Let him rejoice in the works of his hands;
32 He who looks on the earth, and it trembles,
He touches the mountains, and they smoke.
33 I will sing to Jehovah while I live;
I will sing praise to my God while I am in being.
34 Sweet shall be of him my meditation;
I, I will be glad in Jehovah.
35 Sinners shall be consumed from the earth,
And the wicked, they shall be no more.
Bless Jehovah, O my soul.
PRAISE YE JAH.

PSALM CV.

1 Give thanks to Jehovah ; call upon his name ;
Make known his deeds among the peoples.
2 Sing to him, sing praise to him ;
Talk of all his wondrous works.
3 Glory in his holy name ;
Let the heart of them that seek Jehovah rejoice.
4 Seek after Jehovah and his strength ;
Seek his face evermore.
5 Remember his wonders that he has wrought,
His portents, and the judgments of his mouth.
6 Seed of Abraham his servant,
Sons of Jacob, his chosen ones,
7 He, Jehovah, is our God,
His judgments are in all the earth.
8 He remembers his covenant forever,
The word he commanded, to a thousand generations :
9 Which he ratified with Abraham,
And his oath to Isaac ;
10 And confirmed it to Jacob for a statute,
To Israel for an everlasting covenant ;
11 Saying : To thee will I give the land of Canaan,
The portion of your inheritance ;
12 When they were a small number,
Few, and strangers in it.
13 They went from nation to nation,
From one kingdom to another people.
14 He suffered no man to oppress them,
And he reproved kings for their sake [saying] :
15 Touch not my anointed ones,
And to my prophets do no harm.

V. 5. His portents.] Omens of evil, as in the plagues of Egypt, by which his purpose, and his power to execute it, are made known.

V. 9. Ratified with Abraham.] See the impressive ceremonies described in Gen. 15 : 9–17, and the writer's note on the passage.

V. 15. My prophets.] See the use of the word in Gen. 20 : 7.

16 And he called for a famine upon the land;
He broke all the staff of bread.
17 He sent a man before them;
For a servant was Joseph sold.
18 His feet they hurt with fetters,
He was laid in irons;
19 Until the time that his word came;
The saying of Jehovah had cleared him.
20 The king sent and freed him,
The ruler of the peoples, and loosed him.
21 He made him lord of his house,
And ruler over all his substance;
22 To bind his princes at his pleasure,
And teach his elders wisdom.
23 And Israel came into Egypt,
And Jacob sojourned in the land of Ham.
24 And he made his people fruitful exceedingly,
And made them stronger than their foes.

V. 18. He was laid in irons.] So the Genevan version (1560). King James's version owes this happy expression of the thought, as it does many others, to the Puritan version of the Genevan exiles. See the following paragraph.

Some translate, The iron entered into his soul; as in our earliest English Bible. So Coverdale, 1535, Matthews (Tyndale), 1537, Taverner, about 1541, "The iron pierced his heart;" Cranmer's version, 1540 (perpetuated in the Book of Common Prayer), and the Bishops' Bible, 1568, "The iron entered into his soul."*

V. 19. His word came.] To the ear of Pharaoh; was reported to him. Compare Gen. 40 : 14, "make mention of me to Pharaoh," with chap. 41 : 9-13.

V. 19, 2d member. The saying of Jehovah.] What Jehovah said through him (Gen. 40 : 8, "do not interpretations belong to God?") thus owning him for his servant, and approving him as righteous.

V. 22. Elders.] High officers of state; a title of official dignity and rank. Compare Gen. 50 : 7, 8, and the writer's note on the passage.

* There is a grammatical difficulty in this construction and rendering, found in very ancient versions (the Chaldee Targum and the Latin Vulgate), though it may be obviated on plausible grounds. (*Hitzig*, and *Delitzsch*, 2d edition, on the passage.) But the phrase so rendered, striking and beautiful as it is in thought and expression, seems to be less pertinent in the connection.

25 He turned their heart to hate his people,
To plot against his servants.
26 He sent Moses, his servant,
Aaron whom he had chosen.
27 They set his signs among them,
And portents in the land of Ham.
28 He sent darkness, and he made it dark;
And they rebelled not against his words.
29 He turned their waters to blood,
And caused their fish to die.
30 Their land swarmed with frogs,—
In the chambers of their kings.
31 He said, and there came flies,
Lice, in all their border.
32 He gave them hail for rain,
Flaming fire in their land;
33 And smote their vines and their fig-trees,
And broke the trees of their border.
34 He said, and there came locusts,
And caterpillars, and without number;
35 And devoured every herb in their land,
And devoured the fruit of their ground.
36 And he smote all the first-born in their land.
The firstlings of all their strength.
37 And he brought them out with silver and gold;
And there was not a feeble one among his tribes.

V. 27. Set his signs.] As enduring memorials in the history of the people. See the remarks on Ps. 78 : 43.

V. 27, 2d member. Portents.] See the remark on v. 5.

V. 28. Sent darkness.] Here, as in Ps. 78 : 44–51, the plagues are not mentioned in their historical order.

V. 28, 2d member. They.] Moses and Aaron, who are the subject of the verb here, as in the preceding verse. "They set his signs;" and when he "sent darkness" by them, "They rebelled not against his words," as at Meribah (Num. 20 : 24, "ye rebelled against my word at the water of Meribah"), but executed his command with literal exactness.

V. 36. Firstlings of—their strength.] See the same phrase in Gen. 49 : 3, and the writer's note on it.

38 Egypt was glad wnen they went out,
For their dread had fallen upon them.
39 He spread a cloud for a coverin
And fire to give light in the night.
40 They asked, and he brought quails,
And satisfied them with the bread of heaven.
41 He opened the rock, and waters flowed;
They ran in the deserts, a river.
42 For he remembered his holy word,
Abraham his servant;
43 And brought out his people with joy,
His chosen ones with triumph;
44 And gave them the lands of nations,
And the labor of peoples they inherit;
45 That they might keep his statutes,
And observe his laws.
Bless ye JAH.

PSALM CVI.

1 BLESS ye JAH.
Give thanks to Jehovah, for he is good;
For his mercy is forever.
2 Who shall utter the mighty deeds of Jehovah;
Shall cause all his praise to be heard?
3 Happy they that keep judgment,
He that does righteousness at all times.
4 Remember me, Jehovah, with thy favor to thy people;
Visit me with thy salvation.
5 That I may witness the welfare of thy chosen ones,
May rejoice in the gladness of thy nation,
May glory with thy heritage.
6 We have sinned, with our fathers;
We have acted perversely, we have done wickedly.
7 Our fathers in Egypt did not consider thy wonders;
They remembered not the multitude of thy mercies,
And they rebelled by the sea, at the Red Sea.

8 But he saved them for his name's sake,
To make known his might.
9 And he rebuked the Red Sea, and it dried up;
And he made them go through the depths, as in the wilderness.
10 And he saved them out of the hand of the hater,
And redeemed them out of the hand of the enemy.
11 And the waters covered their foes;
Not one of them was left.
12 And they believed his words,
They sang his praise.
13 They made haste to forget his doings;
They waited not for his counsel.
14 They had greedy longings in the wilderness,
And they tempted God in the desert.
15 And he gave them their request,
And sent leanness in their soul.
16 And they were envious of Moses in the camp,
Of Aaron, the holy one of Jehovah.
17 The earth opened, and swallowed up Dathan,
And covered over the company of Abiram.
18 And fire burned in their company;
A flame consumed the wicked.
19 They made a calf in Horeb,
And worshiped a molten image;
20 And changed their glory,
Into the likeness of an ox that eats grass.
21 They forgot God, who saved them;
Who did great things in Egypt,

V. 13. Made haste.] "Soon," (common English version,) does not express the idea. Their inherent perverseness made haste to show itself.

V. 13, 2d member. His counsel.] His own purpose and plan for their relief.

V. 18. Commonly, and perhaps correctly, understood to refer to Num. 16 : 35, 26 : 10, which may seem to be favored by the use of the word "company," as in the preceding verse. But the Hebrew words are in part repeated from Num. 11 : 1, 3, and their "company" may mean the congregation or assembly of Israel, as often elsewhere.

22 Wondrous things in the land of Ham,
Terrible things by the Red Sea.
23 And he said he would destroy them;
Had not Moses stood in the breach before him,
To turn back his wrath from destroying.
24 And they rejected the pleasant land;
They believed not his word.
25 And they murmured in their tents;
They hearkened not to the voice of Jehovah.
26 And he lifted up his hand to them,
To make them fall in the wilderness;
27 And to make their seed fall among the nations,
And to scatter them in the lands.
28 And they joined themselves to Baal-Peor,
And ate the sacrifices of the dead.
29 And they provoked displeasure by their deeds,
And a plague broke in upon them.
30 Then Phineas stood up, and executed judgment,
And the plague was stayed.
31 And it was reckoned to him for righteousness,
To generation and generation, forevermore.
32 They provoked anger at the waters of Strife;
And it went ill with Moses on their account.
33 For they provoked his spirit,
And he spoke unadvisedly with his lips.
34 They did not destroy the peoples,
Of whom Jehovah told them;
35 But mixed themselves with the heathen,
And learned their works;

V. 26. Lifted up his hand.] In confirmation of an oath; as in Ex. 6 : 8 (properly, "I lifted my hand to give it to Abraham"), Deut. 32 : 40. Compare Gen. 14 : 22.

V. 26, 2d member. The words of the oath (Num. 14 : 29) "Shall fall in this wilderness." They should be retained, therefore, in the version here.

V. 28, 2d member. The dead.] Lifeless idols.

V. 32. Of Strife.] Of Meribah.

36 And they served their idols,
And they became a snare to them.
37 And they sacrificed their sons and their daughters to demons.
38 And they shed innocent blood;
Blood of their sons and their daughters,
Whom they sacrificed to the idols of Canaan;
And the land was polluted with bloodshed.
39 And they were defiled with their works,
And played the harlot in their deeds.
40 And Jehovah's anger was kindled against his people,
And he abhorred his heritage.
41 And he gave them into the hand of the heathen,
And they that hated them ruled over them.
42 And their enemies oppressed them,
And they were bowed down under their hand.
43 Many times would he rescue them;
And they rebelled in their counsel,
And were brought low for their iniquity.
44 But he looked on their distress,
When he heard their cry.
45 And he remembered for them his covenant,
And pitied them according to the abundance of his mercy;
46 And made them objects of compassion,
In presence of all that carried them captive.
47 Save us, Jehovah, our God,
And gather us from the nations;
To give thanks to thy holy name,
To glory in thy praise.

BLESSED BE JEHOVAH, GOD OF ISRAEL,
FROM EVERLASTING, AND TO EVERLASTING.
AND LET ALL THE PEOPLE SAY, AMEN.
PRAISE YE JAH.

V. 39, 2d member Compare the remark on Ps. 73 : 27.

V. 43. Their counsel.] What they devised and planned for themselves, without regard to Jehovah's purposes and will.

FIFTH BOOK.

PSALM CVII.

1 Give thanks to Jehovah, for he is good;
For his mercy is forever.
2 Let the redeemed of Jehovah say it,
Whom he redeemed from the hand of the foe;
3 And gathered them out of the lands,
From the east and from the west, from the north and from the south.
4 They wandered in the wilderness, in a desert way;
They found not a city for a habitation.
5 Hungry and thirsty,
Their soul fainted in them.
6 Then they cried to Jehovah in their trouble,
And he rescued them out of their distresses.
7 And he led them by a straight way,
That they might go to a city for a habitation.
8 Let them give thanks to Jehovah for his mercy,
And his wonderful works to the sons of men.
9 For he satisfies the longing soul,
And the hungry soul he fills with good.
10 As they sat in darkness and the shadow of death,
Bound in affliction and iron;—
11 Because they rebelled against the words of the Mighty One,
And contemned the counsel of the Most High,
12 And he bowed down their heart with trouble,
They stumbled, and there was none to help;—
13 Then they cried to Jehovah in their strait,
And he saved them out of their distresses.

14 He brought them out from darkness and the shadow of death,
And broke their bands asunder.
15 Let them give thanks to Jehovah for his mercy,
And his wonderful works to the sons of men.
16 For he has broken the doors of brass,
And cut the bars of iron asunder.
17 Fools, because of their way of transgression,
And because of their iniquities, bring affliction on themselves.
18 All food their soul abhors,
And they draw near unto the gates of death.
19 Then they cry to Jehovah in their strait,
And he saves them out of their distresses.
20 He sends his word, and heals them,
And delivers them from their pits.
21 Let them give thanks to Jehovah for his mercy,
And his wonderful works to the sons of men.
22 And let them sacrifice the sacrifices of thanksgiving,
And recount his works with rejoicing.
23 They that go down to the sea in ships,
That do business in great waters;
24 These see the works of Jehovah,
And his wonders in the deep.
25 For he spoke, and raised a stormy wind,
And it lifted up the waves thereof.
26 They mount up to the heavens, they go down to the abysses;
Their soul is melted because of trouble.
27 They reel and stagger like a drunken man,
And all their wisdom comes to naught.
28 Then they cry to Jehovah in their strait,
And he brings them out of their distresses.

V. 20. Their pits.] Intended for them, and into which they are about to fall.

V. 24. His wonders.] Such as are spoken of in the following verses.

29 He hushes the storm to silence,
And the waves thereof are still.
30 Then are they glad, because they are at rest,
And he leads them to their desired haven.
31 Let them give thanks to Jehovah for his mercy,
And his wonderful works to the sons of men.
32 And let them exalt him in the congregation of the people,
And praise him in the assembly of the elders.
33 He turns rivers into a wilderness,
And water-springs into dry ground;
34 A fruitful land into barrenness,
For the wickedness of them that dwell therein.
35 He turns the wilderness into a pool of water,
And a dry land into water-springs.
36 And there he makes the hungry dwell,
And they found a city for a habitation.
37 And they sow fields, and plant vineyards,
And produce fruits of the [yearly] increase.
38 And he blesses them, and they multiply greatly,
And their cattle he makes not few.
39 And they become few, and are brought low,
From oppression, suffering, and sorrow;
40 He pours contempt upon princes,
And makes them wander in a pathless waste.
41 And he sets the needy on high out of affliction,
And makes families like a flock.
42 The upright shall see, and rejoice,
And all iniquity stop her mouth.
43 Whoso is wise, let him observe these things;
And let them attentively consider the mercies of Jehovah.

V. 30. They are at rest.] The waves are meant. Such alternations of the subject, expressed by a pronoun, are frequent in Hebrew, and can not be avoided in translation.

V. 43. Some translate these words as a question, but less pertinently in the connection:

Who is wise, and will observe these things,
And will attentively consider the mercies of Jehovah?

PSALM CVIII.

A Song. A Psalm of David.

1 My heart is fixed, O God;
I will sing, and will sing praise,—my glory also.
2 Awake lute and harp;
I will awake the dawn!
3 I will praise thee among the peoples, O Jehovah;
I will sing praise to thee among the nations.
4 For great above the heavens is thy mercy,
And unto the clouds thy truth.
5 Be thou exalted above the heavens, O God,
And thy glory over all the earth!
6 That thy beloved ones may be delivered,
Save with thy right hand, and answer me.
7 God has spoken in his holiness. I will triumph;
I will divide Shechem, and will mete out the valley of Succoth.
8 Gilead is mine, Manasseh is mine,
And Ephraim is the defense of my head;
Judah is my ruler's staff.
9 Moab is my wash-basin;
Upon Edom will I cast my shoe;
Over Philistia will I shout aloud.
10 Who will conduct me to the fortified city?
Who has led me unto Edom?
11 Hast not thou, O God, cast us off,
And wilt not go forth, O God, with our armies?
12 Give us help from the foe;
For vain is the deliverance of man.
13 Through God we will do valiantly,
And he it is that will tread down our foes.

V. 1. My glory.] What is noblest in man, and is his true glory,—his spiritual nature.—My glory also.] Shall accompany the outward expression of praise in music and song. Compare Ps. 57 : 8, "Awake, my glory."

PSALM CIX.

To the Chief Musician. A Psalm of David.

1 God of my praise, be not silent!
2 For a wicked mouth, and a mouth of deceit, have they opened against me;
They have spoken against me with a tongue of falsehood.
3 And with words of hatred they have compassed me,
And have fought against me without cause.
4 In return for my love they are my adversaries;
But I give myself to prayer.
5 And they laid upon me evil in return for good,
And hatred in return for my love.
6 Appoint thou over him a wicked one,
And let an adversary stand at his right hand,
7 When he is judged, let him go forth guilty,
And let his prayer become sin.
8 Let his days be few;
His office let another take.
9 Let his sons be orphans,
And his wife a widow.
10 Let his sons continually wander and beg,
And seek [help] far from their ruins.
11 Let the usurer lay a snare for all that he has,
And let strangers despoil his labor.
12 Let him have no one to extend mercy,
And let there be none to show favor to his orphans.
13 Let his posterity be cut off;
In the generation following let their name be blotted out.
14 Let the iniquity of his fathers be in remembrance with Jehovah,
And let not the sin of his mother be blotted out.

VV. 6–20. See the note on Ps. 69 : 22–28.

V. 6. At his right hand.] The position of the accuser.

V. 10. Their ruins.] Their ruined homes.

15 Let them be before Jehovah continually,
And let him cut off their memory from the earth.
16 Because he remembered not to show mercy,
And persecuted a man afflicted and needy,
And stricken in heart, to slay him.
17 And he loved cursing, and it came upon him;
And he delighted not in blessing,
And it was far from him.
18 And he put on cursing as his garment;
And it came like water into his bowels,
And like oil into his bones.
19 Let it be to him as the robe he wears,
And for a belt let him always gird it on.
20 Let this be the reward of my adversaries from Jehovah,
And of them that speak evil against my soul.
21 And thou, Jehovah, Lord,
Do for me, for the sake of thy name.
For good is thy mercy; rescue me.
22 For I am afflicted and needy,
And my heart is pierced within me.
23 Like the shadow, as it lengthens, I am passing away;
I am driven away like the locust.
24 My knees falter through fasting,
And my flesh pines away from [its] fatness.
25 And I am become to them a reproach;
They see me, they shake their head.
26 Help me, Jehovah, my God,
Save me, according to thy mercy.
27 And they shall know that this is thy hand;
Thou, Jehovah, hast done it.
28 They will curse, and thou wilt bless;
They have risen up, and shall be shamed, and thy servant will rejoice.

V. 23. Like the shadow, as it lengthens.] As the lengthening of the shadow shows that it will soon vanish away.

V. 23, 2d member. Like the locust.] Locusts are always driven before the wind. Compare Ex. 10 : 13 and 19.

29 My adversaries shall be clothed with shame,
And cover themselves with their confusion as with a robe.
30 I will thank Jehovah greatly with my mouth,
And in the midst of many will I praise him.
31 For he will stand on the right hand of the needy,
To save him from them that judge his soul.

PSALM CX.

A Psalm of David.

1 JEHOVAH said to my Lord: Sit thou at my right hand,
Till I shall make thy enemies a stool for thy feet.
2 The rod of thy strength will Jehovah stretch forth from Zion;
Rule thou in the midst of thy enemies.
3 Thy people are free-will offerings in the day of thy warfare, in beauties of holiness;
From the womb of the morning thou hast thy dew of youth.
4 Jehovah has sworn, and he will not repent:
Thou art a priest forever, after the order of Melchizedek.
5 The Lord is on thy right hand;
He smites kings in the day of his anger.

V. 31. On the right hand.] To aid and defend, as in Ps. 110 : 5.

V. 1. Stool for thy feet.] More emphatic than footstool, Ps. 99 : 5, where the Hebrew has another form.

V. 3. In beauties of holiness.] Sanctified for the holy warfare. There may be a typical reference in the ceremonial purity of the person and garments. Compare Ex. 19 : 10; and for the spiritual meaning, Pss. 29 : 2, 96 : 9.

V. 3, 2d member. A latent comparison, intimated but not fully expressed. "Dew of youth" suggests the freshness and beauty of young life. "Womb of the morning" suggests the prolific source of the countless dew-drops. Accordingly, "From the womb of the morning thou hast thy dew of youth," suggests the countless numbers and fresh vigor of the youthful warriors, as the dew-drops poured forth from the womb of the morning.

V. 5. On thy right hand.] For aid and defense, as in Ps. 109 : 31.

6 He will judge among the heathen ; he fills with dead bodies ;
He smites the head, over broad lands.
7 Of the brook, in the way, will he drink,
Therefore will he lift up the head.

PSALM CXI.

1 PRAISE YE JAH.
I will thank Jehovah with the whole heart,
In the company of the upright and in the congregation.
2 Great are the works of Jehovah,
Searched out by all that delight in them.
3 Honorable and glorious is his work,
And his righteousness stands fast forever.
4 He has made a memorial for his wonderful works ;
Gracious and compassionate is Jehovah.
5 The prey he has given to them that fear him ;
He will forever remember his covenant.
6 The might of his works he has shown to his people,
To give to them the heritage of the nations.
7 The works of his hand are truth and judgment ;
Sure are all thy precepts ;
8 Established forever and ever,
Done in truth and uprightness.
9 Redemption has he sent to his people ;
He commanded his covenant forever.
Holy and fearful is his name.
10 The beginning of wisdom is the fear of Jehovah.
A good understanding have all they that do them.
His praise endures forever.

V. 7. Of the brook, in the way.] Not pausing, in the pursuit, for further refreshment, and re-invigorated by this chance supply. This Messianic Psalm represents a warrior king, going forth "conquering and to conquer" (Rev. 6 : 2), and all the imagery is in accordance with this conception. Hence this trait of hardihood and endurance, in the pursuit of the routed and flying foe.

V. 10, 2d member. Them.] His precepts (v. 7).

PSALM CXII.

1 Praise ye Jah.
Happy the man that fears Jehovah,
That delights greatly in his commandments.
2 Mighty in the earth shall be his seed;
The generation of the upright shall be blessed.
3 Wealth and riches are in his house;
And his righteousness stands fast forever.
4 There has risen in the darkness a light for the upright,
Gracious, and compassionate, and righteous.
5 Happy is the man that shows favor and lends;
He maintains his cause in the judgment.
6 For he shall not be moved forever;
The righteous will be in everlasting remembrance.
7 He shall not be afraid of evil tidings;
His heart is fixed, trusting in Jehovah.
8 His heart is established, he shall not be afraid,
Until he shall see his desire on his foes.
9 He has dispersed, he has given to the needy;
His righteousness stands fast forever.
His horn shall be exalted in honor.
10 The wicked shall see it, and be vexed;
He will gnash his teeth, and melt away.
The desire of the wicked shall perish.

PSALM CXIII.

1 Praise ye Jah.
Praise, ye servants of Jehovah,
Praise the name of Jehovah.
2 Let the name of Jehovah be blessed,
Henceforth, and forever.

V. 5. Lends.] In charity, to the poor. Compare v. 9, and Prov. 19 : 17.

3 From the rising of the sun until its going down,
Praised be the name of Jehovah.
4 High above all nations is Jehovah;
Above the heavens is his glory.
5 Who is like Jehovah, our God,
He that sits on high;
6 He that looks far down,
On the heavens and on the earth?
7 He raises up the weak out of the dust;
He lifts up the needy from the dunghill;
8 To make him sit with nobles,
With the nobles of his people.
9 He makes the barren dwell in the family,
The rejoicing mother of sons.
PRAISE YE JAH.

PSALM CXIV.

1 WHEN Israel went forth out of Egypt,
The house of Jacob from a people of strange language;
2 Judah became his sanctuary,
Israel his dominion.
3 The sea saw, and fled;
The Jordan turned back.
4 The mountains leaped like rams,
Hills like the young of the flock.
5 What ails thee, thou sea, that thou fleest?
Thou Jordan, that thou turnest back?
6 Ye mountains, that ye leap like rams,
Hills, like young of the flock?
7 Tremble thou earth, before the Lord,
Before the God of Jacob;
Who turned the rock into a pool of water,
The flinty rock into a fountain of waters.

V. 9. In the family.] A family of her own. The blessing most prized and sought, the family relation of mother and children.

PSALM CXV.

1 Not unto us, O Jehovah, not unto us,
But to thy name, give glory,
For thy mercy, for thy truth.
2 Wherefore should the heathen say:
Where now is their God?
3 But our God is in the heavens;
All that he pleased he has done.
4 Their idols are silver and gold,
The work of the hands of man.
5 A mouth have they, but they speak not;
Eyes have they, but they see not.
6 Ears have they, but they hear not;
A nose have they, but they smell not.
7 Their hands,—they handle not;
Their feet,—they walk not.
They make no sound in their throat.
8 Like to them are they that make them,
Every one that trusts in them.
9 Israel, trust thou in Jehovah;
He is their help and their shield.
10 House of Aaron, trust ye in Jehovah;
He is their help and their shield.
11 Ye that fear Jehovah, trust in Jehovah;
He is their help and their shield.
12 Jehovah has been mindful of us; he will bless;
Will bless the house of Israel,
Will bless the house of Aaron;
13 Will bless them that fear Jehovah,
The small with the great.
14 Jehovah add to you,
To you and to your children!
15 Blessed be ye of Jehovah,
Maker of heaven and earth.

16 The heavens are Jehovah's heavens;
And the earth he has given to the sons of men.
17 The dead praise not JAH,
And none that go down to silence.
18 But we will bless JAH,
Henceforth, and forever.
PRAISE YE JAH.

PSALM CXVI.

1 I LOVE—because Jehovah hears
My voice and my supplications;
2 Because he has inclined his ear to me,
And I will call while I live.
3 The bands of death encompassed me,
And the pangs of the underworld came upon me.
I find trouble and sorrow.
4 And I call on the name of Jehovah:
Jehovah, I pray, deliver my soul!
5 Gracious is Jehovah, and righteous;
And our God shows compassion.
6 Jehovah preserves the simple;
I was brought low, and he helped me.
7 Return, my soul, to thy rest,
For Jehovah has dealt bountifully with thee.
8 For thou hast rescued my soul from death,
My eyes from tears,
My feet from falling.
9 I will walk before Jehovah,
In the lands of the living.

V. 17. Silence.] Of the grave; as in Ps. 94 : 17.

V. 9. In the lands of the living.] In Ps. 27 : 13 is the more restricted expression, "in the land of the living." Here the meaning is, in whatever lands, wherever my lot may fall.

10 I believed, for [so] I speak.
I, I was afflicted greatly.
11 I said in my alarm,
All mankind are false.
12 How shall I repay to Jehovah,
All his benefits bestowed upon me?
13 I will take the cup of salvation,
And will call on the name of Jehovah.
14 I will pay my vows to Jehovah,
Yea, in the presence of all his people.
15 Precious in the eyes of Jehovah
Is the death of his saints.
16 I beseech, O Jehovah—for I am thy servant,
I am thy servant, the son of thy handmaid;
Thou hast loosed my bonds.
17 To thee will I offer a sacrifice of thanksgiving,
And will call on the name of Jehovah.
18 I will pay my vows to Jehovah,
Yea, in the presence of all his people;
19 In the courts of the house of Jehovah,
In the midst of thee, O Jerusalem.
PRAISE YE JAH.

PSALM CXVII.

1 PRAISE Jehovah, all ye nations;
Extol him, all ye peoples.
2 For great is his mercy toward us;
And the truth of Jehovah is forever.
PRAISE YE JAH.

V. 10. For [so] I speak.] Implying, that he could not speak as he had done, if he had not believed.

V. 11. All mankind are false.] Implying, that God alone is to be trusted.

VV. 12, 13. The question and answer imply, that "his benefits" can not be repaid.

PSALM CXVIII.

1 GIVE thanks to Jehovah, for he is good;
For his mercy is forever.
2 Let Israel say,—
For his mercy is forever.
3 Let the house of Aaron say,—
For his mercy is forever.
4 Let them that fear Jehovah say,—
For his mercy is forever.
5 Out of the anguish I called on JAH;
JAH answered [and set] me in a large place.
6 Jehovah is for me, I will not fear;
What can man do to me?
7 Jehovah is for me, with my helpers,
And I, I shall see my desire on them that hate me.
8 It is better to trust in Jehovah,
Than to confide in man.
9 It is better to trust in Jehovah,
Than to confide in princes.
10 All the heathen compass me about;
In the name of Jehovah I will surely cut them off.
11 They compass me about, yea they surround me;
In the name of Jehovah I will surely cut them off.
12 They compass me about like bees;
They are quenched like the fire of thorns;
In the name of Jehovah I will surely cut them off.
13 Thou didst sorely thrust at me, that I might fall;
But Jehovah helped me.

VV. 2–4. The Psalmist calls on Israel, on the house of Aaron, on all that fear Jehovah, to repeat the ground of thanksgiving, "For his mercy is forever."

V. 5, 2d member. Compare Ps. 31 : 8, "hast set my feet in a large place," and Ps. 18 : 19, "brought me forth to a large place."

V. 12. Like the fire of thorns.] Noisy and brief. Compare Eccl. 7 : 6.

14 JAH is my strength and song,
And he is become my salvation.
15 The voice of triumph and salvation
Is in the tents of the righteous.
The right hand of Jehovah has wrought mightily.
16 The right hand of Jehovah is uplifted high;
The right hand of Jehovah has wrought mightily.
17 I shall not die, but shall live,
And shall recount the works of JAH.
18 JAH has sorely chastened me,
But has not given me over to death.
19 Open to me the gates of righteousness;
I will come in by them, I will give thanks to JAH.
20 This is the gate of Jehovah;
The righteous shall come in by it.
21 I will thank thee that thou hast answered me,
And art become my salvation.
22 The stone which the builders rejected,
Has become the head of the corner.
23 This is from Jehovah;
It is wonderful in our eyes.
24 This is the day Jehovah has made;
We will exult and be glad in it.
25 I beseech, O Jehovah, save now!
I beseech, O Jehovah, send now prosperity!
26 Blessed is he that comes in the name of Jehovah.
We bless you from the house of Jehovah.
27 Mighty is Jehovah, and has given us light.
Bind the festal sacrifice with cords,
Even unto the horns of the altar.
28 Thou art my God, and I will thank thee,
My God, I will exalt thee.
29 Give thanks to Jehovah, for he is good;
For his mercy is forever.

V. 16. Is uplifted high.] *Or*, lifts on high; namely, to a place of safety. Compare Pss. 18 : 48; 91 : 14.

PSALM CXIX.

Aleph.

1 Happy the upright in their way,
Who walk in the law of Jehovah.
2 Happy they that keep his testimonies,
That seek him with the whole heart;
3 Who also do no wrong,
Who walk in his ways.
4 Thou hast enjoined thy precepts,
That we should keep them strictly.
5 O that my ways were directed,
To keep thy statutes.
6 Then shall I not be shamed,
When I have respect to all thy commandments.
7 I will praise thee with uprightness of heart,
While I learn thy righteous judgments.
8 Thy statutes I will keep.
Do not forsake me utterly!

Beth.

9 Whereby shall a young man keep his path pure?
By taking heed according to thy word.
10 With my whole heart have I sought thee;
Do not let me wander from thy commandments.
11 In my heart have I treasured thy saying,
That I may not sin against thee.
12 Blessed be thou, O Jehovah!
Teach me thy statutes.
13 With my lips have I recounted
All the judgments of thy mouth.
14 In the way of thy testimonies have I rejoiced,
As over all riches.

Ps. cxix. Compare Introduction, § 8, second paragraph.

15 In thy precepts will I meditate,
And have respect to thy paths.
16 In thy statutes will I delight myself;
I will not forget thy word.

Gimel.

17 Deal kindly with thy servant that I may live;
And I will keep thy word.
18 Open thou mine eyes, and let me behold,—
Wondrous things out of thy law!
19 I am a stranger in the earth;
Do not hide from me thy commandments.
20 My soul breaks with longing,
Toward thy judgments at all times.
21 Thou hast rebuked the proud, accursed,
That wander from thy commandments.
22 Roll off from me reproach and contempt;
For thy testimonies have I kept.
23 Also princes sat and talked against me;
Thy servant meditates on thy statutes.
24 Also thy testimonies are my delight,
My counselors.

Daleth.

25 My soul cleaves to the dust;
Do thou revive me according to thy word.
26 My ways I have declared, and thou didst answer me;
Teach me thy statutes.
27 The way of thy precepts make me understand;
And I will meditate on thy wonders.
28 My soul melts away with sorrow;
Raise me up, according to thy word.
29 The way of falsehood remove from me,
And grant me graciously thy law.
30 The way of truth have I chosen;
Thy judgments I have set [before me.]

31 I have cleaved to thy testimonies;
Jehovah, do not put me to shame.
32 The way of thy commandments I will run;
For thou wilt enlarge my heart.

He.

33 Teach me, O Jehovah, the way of thy statutes,
And I will keep it to the end.
34 Make me understand and I will keep thy law,
And will observe it with the whole heart.
35 Make me tread in the path of thy commandments;
For therein do I delight.
36 Incline my heart to thy testimonies,
And not to gain.
37 Turn away my eyes from beholding vanity;
Quicken me in thy way.
38 Confirm to thy servant what thou hast said,
Which is for thy fear.
39 Turn away my reproach which I dread;
For thy judgments are good.
40 Behold, I have longed after thy precepts;
In thy righteousness quicken thou me.

Vav.

41 And let thy mercies come to me, O Jehovah,
Thy salvation, according to thy saying.
42 And I shall answer him that reproaches me;
For I have trusted in thy word.
43 And take not from my mouth the word of truth utterly;
For I have waited for thy judgments.
44 And I will keep thy law continually,
Forever and ever.

V. 38. For thy fear.] To lead men to the fear of God, assuring them of the blessings attending it.

VV. 41–48. In this stanza, the initial letter is the word *and* in Hebrew; hence its recurrence at the beginning of the first line in each couplet.

45 And I shall walk at large ;
For thy precepts have I sought.
46 And I will speak of thy testimonies before kings,
And will not be ashamed.
47 And I will delight myself in thy commandments,
Which I love.
48 And I will lift up my hands to thy commandments,
Which I love,
And will meditate on thy statutes.

Zayin.

49 Remember the word to thy servant,
On which thou hast caused me to hope.
50 This is my comfort in my affliction ;
For thy saying has revived me.
51 Proud ones have greatly derided me ;
From thy law I have not swerved.
52 I remembered thy judgments of old, O Jehovah,
And have consoled myself.
53 Indignation has taken hold of me because of the wicked,
Who forsake thy law.
54 Thy statutes have been my songs,
In the house of my sojournings.
55 I have remembered thy name in the night, O Jehovah,
And have kept thy law.
56 This I have had,
For thy precepts have I kept.

Cheth.

57 Jehovah is my portion, I have said,
That I may keep thy words.
58 I have sought thy favor with the whole heart ;
Be gracious to me according to thy saying.
59 I thought on my ways,
And turned back my feet to thy testimonies.

V. 44. Will lift up my hands] As a symbol, and an expression, of the lifting up of the heart.

60 I made haste and delayed not,
To keep thy commandments.
61 The cords of the wicked were around me;
Thy law I have not forgotten.
62 At midnight will I rise to give thanks to thee,
On account of thy righteous judgments.
63 I am a companion of all that fear thee,
And of them that keep thy precepts.
64 The earth is full of thy mercy, O Jehovah;
Teach me thy statutes.

Teth.

65 Thou hast dealt well with thy servant,
O Jehovah, according to thy word.
66 Teach me good understanding and knowledge;
For I have believed in thy commandments.
67 Before I was afflicted I went astray;
But now I keep thy saying.
68 Thou art good, and doest good;
Teach me thy statutes.
69 The proud have forged a lie against me;
I, with all the heart, will keep thy precepts.
70 Thick, as with fat, is their heart;
As for me, in thy law do I delight.
71 It is good for me that I was afflicted,
That I might learn thy statutes.
72 Better to me is the law of thy mouth,
Than thousands of gold and silver.

Yod.

73 Thy hands made me, and fashioned me;
Make me understand, that I may learn thy commandments.
74 They that fear thee will see me and will rejoice;
For I have hoped in thy word.

V. 70, 1st member. An expression of insensibility, and dullness of moral perception. Compare Ps. 17 : 10; Is. 6 : 10.

75 I know, O Jehovah, that thy judgments are right,
And in faithfulness thou hast afflicted me.
76 Let, I pray, thy mercy be for my comfort,
According to thy saying to thy servant.
77 Let thy compassions come upon me that I may live ;
For thy law is my delight.
78 Let the proud be ashamed, for they wronged me without cause ;
As for me, I meditate on thy precepts.
79 They will turn to me that fear thee,
And that know thy testimonies.
80 Let my heart be perfect in thy statutes,
That I may not be ashamed.

Caph.

81 My soul faints for thy salvation ;
For thy word do I wait.
82 My eyes fail for thy saying,
While I say : When wilt thou comfort me!
83 For I am become like a bottle in the smoke ;
Thy statutes I do not forget.
84 How many are the days of thy servant?
When wilt thou execute judgment on my persecutors?
85 The proud have digged pits for me,
Who are not according to thy law.
86 All thy commandments are faithfulness ;
They persecute me wrongfully ; help thou me.
87 Almost had they consumed me upon earth ;
And I, I forsook not thy precepts.
88 According to thy mercy revive me,
And I will keep the testimony of thy mouth.

Lamed.

89 Forever, O Jehovah,
Thy word is settled in the heavens.
90 To generation and generation is thy faithfulness ;
Thou hast founded the earth, and it stands fast.

91 For thy judgments they stand fast this day;
For all are thy servants.
92 Unless thy law had been my delight,
I should then have perished in my affliction.
93 Forever will I not forget thy precepts;
For with them thou hast quickened me.
94 Thine am I,—save me;
For thy precepts have I sought.
95 The wicked have waited for me to destroy me;
To thy testimonies do I give heed.
96 To all perfection I have seen an end;
Thy commandment is exceeding broad.

Mem.

97 How do I love thy law!
All the day it is my meditation.
98 Thy commandments make me wiser than my enemies;
For forever is it mine.
99 I am become wiser than my teachers;
For thy testimonies are my meditation.
100 I have more understanding than the aged;
For thy precepts have I kept.
101 From every evil path have I withheld my feet,
In order that I may keep thy word.
102 From thy judgments I have not departed,
For thou thyself dost guide me.
103 How sweet to my palate are thy sayings;
More than honey to my mouth!
104 From thy precepts I get understanding;
Therefore do I hate every false path.

Nun.

105 A lamp to my foot is thy word,
And a light to my path.

V. 96. An end.] A limit, or bound.

V. 98, 2d member. It.] Embracing all in one.

106 I have sworn, and have fulfilled it,
To observe thy righteous judgments.
107 I am afflicted very greatly;
O Jehovah, revive me according to thy word.
108 Let the free-will offerings of my mouth be acceptable to thee, O Jehovah;
And teach me thy judgments.
109 My soul is in my hand continually;
But thy law I do not forget.
110 The wicked have laid a snare for me;
But from thy precepts I have not strayed.
111 Thy testimonies have I taken as a heritage forever;
For they are the joy of my heart.
112 I have inclined my heart to perform thy statutes,
Forever, to the end.

Samech.

113 The double-minded I hate,
And thy law I love.
114 My hiding place and my shield art thou;
For thy word do I wait.
115 Depart from me, ye evil-doers;
And I will keep the commandments of my God.
116 Uphold me according to thy saying, and I shall live;
And do not let me be ashamed of my hope.
117 Do thou hold me up, and I shall be saved;
And I will have regard to thy statutes continually.
118 Thou hast made light of all that wander from thy statutes;
For a vain thing is their deceit.
119 As dross thou hast put away all the wicked of the earth;
Therefore do I love thy testimonies.
120 My flesh shudders from dread of thee,
And of thy judgments I am afraid.

V. 113. The double-minded.] Men of divided mind, "halting between two opinions" (1 Kings 18 : 21, where a word from the same root is used); unstable and wavering. Compare James 1 : 8.

Ayin.

121 I have done justice and righteousness;
Thou wilt not leave me to my oppressors.
122 Be surety for thy servant for good;
Do not let the proud oppress me.
123 My eyes fail for thy salvation,
And for thy righteous saying.
124 Deal with thy servant according to thy mercy,
And teach me thy statutes.
125 I am thy servant,—give me understanding,
And I shall know thy statutes.
126 It is time that Jehovah should work;
They have broken thy law.
127 Therefore do I love thy commandments,
Above gold, and above fine gold.
128 Therefore all thy precepts I esteem right;
Every path of falsehood I hate.

Pe.

129 Wonderful are thy testimonies;
Therefore has my soul kept them.
130 The unfolding of thy words gives light,
Making the simple understand.
131 I opened my mouth wide, and panted;
For I longed for thy commandments.
132 Turn to me, and be gracious to me,
As thou art wont to do to them that love thy name.
133 My steps establish by thy word,
And let no iniquity rule over me.
134 Redeem me from the oppression of man;
And I will observe thy precepts.
135 Make thy face to shine upon thy servant,
And teach me thy statutes.
136 My eyes run down with streams of water,
Because they observe not thy law.

VV. 127, 128. Therefore.] In consideration of all that precedes.

Tsade.

137 Righteous art thou, O Jehovah,
And upright in thy judgments.
138 Thou hast enjoined in righteousness thy testimonies,
And in exceeding faithfulness.
139 My zeal consumes me,
Because my foes forget thy words.
140 Pure is thy saying—exceedingly,
And thy servant loves it.
141 Little am I and despised;
Thy precepts I do not forget.
142 Thy righteousness is eternal right,
And thy law is truth.
143 Trouble and anguish have come upon me;
Thy commandments are my delights.
144 Right are thy testimonies forever;
Make me understand, and I shall live.

Koph.

145 I call with the whole heart; answer me, O Jehovah;
Thy statutes I will keep.
146 I call on thee, save me;
And I will observe thy testimonies.
147 I rise early with the dawn, and cry for help;
For thy words do I wait.
148 My eyes anticipate the night-watches,
To meditate on thy saying.
149 Hear my voice according to thy mercy;
O Jehovah, according to thy judgments revive me.
150 Near are they that follow after mischief;
They are far from thy law.
151 Near art thou, O Jehovah,
And all thy commandments are truth.

V. 148. Anticipate the night-watches.] Anticipate their progress; waking unseasonably, before the night-watches are past. Compare Ps. 63 : 6.

152 Long time have I known from thy testimonies,
That thou hast founded them forever.

Resh.

153 See my affliction, and rescue me;
For thy law I have not forgotten.
154 Plead my cause and redeem me;
According to thy saying revive me.
155 Far from the wicked is salvation;
For thy statutes they have not sought.
156 Many are thy compassions, O Jehovah;
According to thy judgments revive me.
157 Many are my persecutors and my foes;
From thy testimonies I have not swerved.
158 I saw the faithless and loathed,
Them that keep not thy saying.
159 See how I love thy precepts;
O Jehovah, according to thy mercy revive me.
160 The sum of thy word is truth;
And every one of thy righteous judgments is forever.

Schin.

161 Princes persecute me without cause;
But at thy words my heart trembles.
162 I rejoice over thy saying,
As one that finds great spoil.
163 Falsehood I hate and abhor;
Thy law do I love.
164 Seven times in the day I praise thee,
On account of thy righteous judgments.
165 Great peace have they that love thy law;
And they have no occasion of stumbling.
166 I have hoped for thy salvation, O Jehovah;
And have done thy commandments.
167 My soul has observed thy testimonies,
And I love them exceedingly.

168 I have observed thy precepts and thy testimonies;
For all my ways are before thee.

Tav.

169 Let my cry come near before thee, O Jehovah;
According to thy word, make me understand.
170 Let my supplication come before thee;
According to thy saying, rescue me.
171 My lips shall pour forth praise;
For thou wilt teach me thy statutes.
172 Let my tongue answer to thy saying,
That all thy commandments are right.
173 Let thy hand be for my help;
For thy precepts have I chosen.
174 I have longed for thy salvation, O Jehovah;
And thy law is my delight.
175 Let my soul live and praise thee;
And let thy judgments help me.
176 I have gone astray like a lost sheep.
Seek thy servant;
For thy commandments I do not forget.

PSALM CXX.

Pilgrim Song.

1 To JEHOVAH, in my distress,
I called and he answered me.
2 O Jehovah, rescue my soul from lying lips,
From a deceitful tongue.
3 What shall he give to thee,
And what shall he do more to thee, deceitful tongue?

Pss. cxx.—cxxxiv. See Introduction, § 6.

V. 3. Compare the form of imprecation, "God do so and more also" (1 Sam. 14 : 44).

4 Sharp arrows of the mighty,
With burning coals of broom!
5 Alas for me, that I sojourn in Mesech,
That I dwell with the tents of Kedar!
6 My soul has long dwelt
With him that hates peace.
7 I am for peace; but when I speak,
They are for war.

PSALM CXXI.

Pilgrim Song.

1 I WILL lift my eyes unto the mountains;
From whence shall my help come?
2 My help is from Jehovah,
Who made heaven and earth.
3 Let him not suffer thy foot to waver;
He that keeps thee, let him not slumber.
4 Behold he will not slumber, and will not sleep,
That keeps Israel.
5 Jehovah is thy keeper;
Jehovah is thy shade on thy right hand.
6 By day the sun shall not smite thee,
Nor the moon by night.
7 Jehovah will keep thee from all evil;
He will keep thy soul.
8 Jehovah will keep thy going out and thy coming in,
Henceforth and forevermore.

V. 4. With burning coals.] Compare Ps. 140 : 10.

Broom.] A plant used as fuel by the natives of the country, and yielding the best coal.

V. 5. Mesech—Kedar.] Put for any restless and warlike communities, of similar character.

Ps. cxxi. An appropriate hymn, for morning or evening worship, as the pilgrims were journeying toward the mountains of Jerusalem (Ps 125 : 2).

PSALM CXXII.

Pilgrim Song of David.

1 I WAS glad when they said to me,
Let us go into the house of Jehovah.
2 Our feet are standing
In thy gates, O Jerusalem;
3 Jerusalem, that art builded,
As a city that is compact together;
4 Whither the tribes go up,
The tribes of JAH,—a testimony for Israel,—
To give thanks to the name of Jehovah.
5 For there are set thrones for judgment,
Thrones of the house of David.
6 Pray for the peace of Jerusalem;
They shall prosper that love thee!
7 Let there be peace within thy rampart,
Prosperity within thy palaces.
8 For my brethren and companion's sakes,
Let me now say: Peace be within thee!
9 For the sake of the house of Jehovah our God,
I will seek thy good.

PSALM CXXIII.

Pilgrim Song.

1 UNTO thee do I lift up my eyes,
Thou that dwellest in the heavens.
2 Behold, as the eyes of servants are toward the hand of their masters,

---

V. 4. The tribes go up.] "Three times in a year" (Deut. 16 : 16; compare Ex. 23 : 14-17). These annual pilgrimages were "a testimony for Israel,"—"a memorial" (as expressed in Ex. 12 : 14) of what God had wrought.

As the eyes of a maid-servant toward the hand of her mistress ;
So are our eyes toward Jehovah, our God,
Until he shall be gracious to us.
3 Be gracious to us, O Jehovah, be gracious to us ;
For we are greatly filled with contempt.
4 Our soul is greatly filled,
With the scorn of them that are at ease,
With the contempt of the proud.

PSALM CXXIV.

Pilgrim Song of David.

1 If it were not Jehovah who was for us,—
Let Israel now say,—
2 If it were not Jehovah who was for us,
When man rose up against us ;
3 Then had they swallowed us up alive,
When their anger was kindled against us ;
4 Then had the waters overwhelmed us,
The stream had gone over our soul ;
5 Then had gone over our soul
The swelling waters.
6 Blessed be Jehovah,
Who has not given us a prey to their teeth.
7 Our soul is as a bird escaped from the snare of the fowlers ;
The snare is broken and we are escaped.
8 Our help is in the name of Jehovah,
Who made heaven and earth.

Ps. cxxiii. 2, 2d member. Toward the hand of her mistress.] Watching for the signal of her will. The Orientals were always, as they now are, sparing of words, and expressed their will by signs. There is no reference to chastisement, as some suppose.

VV. 3, 4. For the circumstances here referred to, compare Neh. 1 : 3, and 2 : 19.

PSALM CXXV.

Pilgrim Song.

1 THEY that trust in Jehovah are as Mount Zion,
That can not be moved, abides forever.
2 Jerusalem, mountains are round about her;
And Jehovah is round about his people,
Henceforth and forever.
3 For the rod of wickedness shall not rest on the lot of the righteous,
That the righteous may not put forth their hands to iniquity.
4 Do good, O Jehovah, to the good,
To the upright in their hearts.
5 And they that turn aside to their crooked paths,
Jehovah will lead them away with workers of iniquity.
Peace be upon Israel!

PSALM CXXVI.

Pilgrim Song.

1 WHEN Jehovah brought back the returned of Zion,
We were as they that dream.
2 Then was our mouth filled with laughter,
And our tongue with singing.
Then said they among the heathen:
Jehovah has done great things for them.
3 Jehovah has done great things for us;
We are joyful.
4 Turn, O Jehovah, our captivity,
As streams in the south.
5 They that sow in tears shall reap in joy.
6 He goes forth weeping as he goes, bearing the handful of seed;
He shall surely come with rejoicing, bearing his sheaves.

V. 4. A prayer for the continuation of the work to its completion.

PSALM CXXVII.

Pilgrim Song of Solomon.

1 If Jehovah build not the house,
In vain they labor upon it that build it.
If Jehovah keep not the city,
The keeper watches in vain.
2 Vain is it for you, that ye rise early,
That ye take rest late,
That ye eat the bread of sorrows;
So gives he to his beloved in sleep.
3 Lo, sons are a heritage from Jehovah;
The fruit of the womb is a reward.
4 As arrows in the hand of a mighty man,
So are the sons of youth.
5 Happy the man,
Who has filled his quiver with them.
They shall not be ashamed,
When they shall speak with enemies in the gate.

PSALM CXXVIII.

Pilgrim Song.

1 Happy is every one that fears Jehovah,
That walks in his ways.
2 For thou shalt eat of the labor of thy hands;
Happy art thou, and it is well with thee!

V. 2, 4th member. So, all that is thus gained, he gives in sleep, without this care and pains.

V. 5, 4th member. Enemies.] Personal enemies are probably meant, whom they would "speak with in the gate;" namely, the broad open space at the gate of the city, where men met for the transaction of business, and magistrates sat to administer justice. See the note on Ps. 55 : 11, and compare Job 5 : 4 (and the references in the writer's note) and 29 : 7.

3 Thy wife, as a fruitful vine,
In the interior of thy house;
Thy sons, as olive-plants,
Around thy table!
4 Behold, thus shall the man be blest,
That fears Jehovah.
5 Jehovah will bless thee out of Zion;
And thou shalt see the good of Jerusalem,
All the days of thy life.
6 And thou shalt see thy children's children.
Peace be upon Israel!

PSALM CXXIX.

Pilgrim Song.

1 MUCH have they oppressed me from my youth,—
Let Israel now say,—
2 Much have they oppressed me from my youth,
Yet have they not prevailed against me.
3 Ploughers ploughed upon my back;
They made long their furrows.
4 Jehovah, the righteous,
Has cut asunder the cords of the wicked.
5 Let them be shamed, and be turned back, all that hate Zion.
6 Let them be as grass on the house-tops,
That withers before it is plucked up.
7 With which the mower fills not his hand,
Nor the gatherer his arm.
8 And they that pass by say not:
The blessing of Jehovah be upon you;
We bless you in the name of Jehovah.

V. 3. In the interior.] The women's apartments were the most retired part of the house.

V. 8, 2d and 3d members. Compare the salutation in Ruth 2 : 4.

PSALM CXXX.

Pilgrim Song.

1 Out of the depths I call on thee, Jehovah.
2 Lord, hearken to my voice ;
Let thine ears be attentive,
To the voice of my supplications.
3 If thou, O Jah, shouldst mark iniquities,
O Lord, who shall stand?
4 For with thee there is forgiveness,
That thou mayest be feared.
5 I have waited for Jehovah, my soul has waited ;
And in his word have I hoped.
6 My soul [waits] for the Lord,
More than they that watch, for the morning,—
Than they that watch, for the morning!
7 Hope thou, Israel, in Jehovah ;
For with Jehovah there is mercy,
And with him abundant redemption.
8 And he, he will redeem Israel,
From all his iniquities.

PSALM CXXXI.

Pilgrim Song of David.

1 Jehovah, my heart is not haughty,
Nor my eyes lofty ;
Nor do I concern myself with things too great,
And with things too difficult for me.

V. 4. For with thee there is forgiveness.] Referring to what is implied in v. 3 ; namely, a motive in the divine mind for relaxing the rigor of the divine law. The motive is, that men may be led to fear God by the hope of pardon and acceptance, without which none would be reclaimed.

V. 6, 2d and 3d members. The meaning is not, watch for the morning,—as some understand it,—but wait for the morning, as indicated by the proper punctuation.

2 But I have calmed and quieted my spirit,
As a weaned child on its mother;
As the weaned child is my spirit within me.
3 Hope thou, Israel, in Jehovah,
Henceforth and forever.

PSALM CXXXII.

Pilgrim Song.

1 JEHOVAH, remember to David all his pains;
2 Who did swear unto Jehovah,
Did vow to the mighty one of Jacob:
3 I will not enter into the tent of my house,
I will not go up on the couch of my bed;
4 I will not give sleep to my eyes,
Slumber to my eyelids;
5 Until I shall find a place for Jehovah,
Dwellings for the mighty one of Jacob.
6 Lo, we heard of it at Ephratah;
We found it in the wooded fields.
7 We will enter in to his dwellings,
We will worship at his footstool.
8 Arise, O Jehovah, to thy resting-place,
Thou, and the ark of thy strength.
9 Let thy priests be clothed with righteousness,
And let thy saints shout for joy.
10 For the sake of David thy servant,
Do not turn back the face of thine anointed.

V. 3. Tent of my house.] My temporary dwelling; a reminiscence of patriarchal times, perpetuated in the language, and a reminder that our brief earthly life is but a sojourn and a pilgrimage.

V. 5. Dwellings.] As in Ps. 46 : 4, 84 : 1.

V. 6, 2d member. Wooded fields.] Compare Kirjath-jearim (city of the woods) 1 Sam. 7 : 1, and 2 Sam. 6 : 2, where it is called Baale (Josh. 15 : 9)

VV. 8–10. Compare 2 Chron. 6 : 41, 42.

11 Jehovah has sworn to David in truth,
He will not turn back from it:
Of the fruit of thy body will I set upon thy throne.
12 If thy sons will observe my covenant,
And my testimonies that I shall teach them;
Also their sons forever
Shall sit upon thy throne.
13 For Jehovah has chosen Zion;
He has desired it for his abode.
14 This is my resting-place forever;
Here will I dwell, for I have desired it.
15 Her provision I will abundantly bless;
Her needy I will satisfy with bread.
16 And her priests will I clothe with salvation,
And her saints shall shout aloud for joy.
17 There will I cause the horn of David to put forth;
I have prepared a lamp for my anointed.
18 His enemies will I clothe with shame;
But on him shall his crown flourish.

PSALM CXXXIII.

Pilgrim Song of David.

1 Behold, how good, and how pleasant,
The dwelling of brethren in union!
2 As the precious oil upon the head,
Flowing down upon the beard,
The beard of Aaron,
That flowed down to the border of his vestments!

V. 17. To put forth.] New branches; an emblem of increasing power. Compare Ezek. 29 : 21.

V. 18. Shall his crown flourish.] Said of the wreath or chaplet, with which the victor was crowned. If "crown" is here the common symbol of sovereignty, the meaning is, shall prosper, shall suffer no reverse. Contrast the language of Ps 89 : 39.

3 As the dew of Hermon,
That comes down on the mountains of Zion!
For there Jehovah commanded the blessing,
Life forevermore.

PSALM CXXXIV.

Pilgrim Song.

1 BEHOLD, bless ye Jehovah,
All ye servants of Jehovah,
That stand in the house of Jehovah by night.
2 Lift up your hands toward the sanctuary,
And bless Jehovah.
3 Jehovah bless thee out of Zion,
Maker of heaven and earth.

PSALM CXXXV.

1 PRAISE ye JAH.
Praise ye the name of Jehovah;
Praise, ye servants of Jehovah,
2 That stand in the house of Jehovah,
In the courts of the house of our God.
3 Praise ye JAH, for Jehovah is good;
Sing praise to his name, for it is pleasant.
4 For JAH has chosen Jacob for himself,
Israel for his peculiar treasure.
5 For I know that Jehovah is great,
And our Lord above all gods.
6 All that Jehovah pleased he has done,
In the heavens and on earth,
In the seas and all depths.

V. 3. Dew of Hermon.] Compare Dr. Hackett's remarks, in the American edition of *Smith's Bible Dictionary*, art. Hermon, Dew of, p. 1048.

V. 4. His peculiar treasure.] For the meaning, see Ex. 19 : 5.

7 Who causes vapors to ascend from the end of the earth,
Makes lightnings for the rain,
Brings out the wind from his storehouses.
8 Who smote the first-born of Egypt,
Both of man and beast;
9 Sent signs and portents in thy midst, O Egypt,
On Pharaoh and on his servants.
10 Who smote many nations,
And slew mighty kings;
11 Sihon, king of the Amorites,
And Og, king of Bashan,
And all the kingdoms of Canaan;
12 And gave their land as a heritage,
A heritage to Israel his people.
13 Jehovah, thy name is forever;
Jehovah, thy memorial is to all generations.
14 For Jehovah will judge his people,
And for the sake of his servants will repent.
15 The idols of the heathen are silver and gold,
The work of the hands of man.
16 A mouth have they, but they speak not;
Eyes have they, but they see not.
17 Ears have they, but they hear not;
Yea, there is no breath in their mouth.
18 Like to them are they that make them,
Every one that trusts in them.
19 House of Israel, bless ye Jehovah;
House of Aaron, bless ye Jehovah;
20 House of Levi, bless ye Jehovah;
Ye that fear Jehovah, bless Jehovah.
21 Blessed be Jehovah out of Zion,
Who inhabits Jerusalem.
Praise ye JAH.

V. 9. Portents.] See the remark on Ps. 105 : 5.

V. 13. Memorial.] Memorial name. See the remark on Ps. 30 : 4.

V. 14. See Deut. 32 : 36, from which these words are taken.

VV. 15–18. Repeated, with slight variations, from Ps. 115 : 4–8.

PSALM CXXXVI.

1 Give thanks to Jehovah, for he is good;
For his mercy is forever.
2 Give thanks to the God of gods;
For his mercy is forever.
3 Give thanks to the Lord of lords;
For his mercy is forever.
4 To him who alone doeth great wonders;
For his mercy is forever.
5 To him who made the heavens with skill;
For his mercy is forever.
6 To him who spread out the earth upon the waters;
For his mercy is forever.
7 To him who made great lights;
For his mercy is forever;
8 The sun for dominion over the day;
For his mercy is forever;
9 The moon and stars for dominion over the night;
For his mercy is forever.
10 To him who smote Egypt in their first-born;
For his mercy is forever;
11 And brought out Israel from their midst;
For his mercy is forever;
12 With a strong hand and an outstretched arm,
For his mercy is forever.
13 To him who divided the Red Sea into parts;
For his mercy is forever
14 And made Israel pass through in the midst of it;
For his mercy is forever;
15 And shook out Pharaoh and his host into the Red Sea;
For his mercy is forever.
16 To him who led his people in the wilderness;
For his mercy is forever.

V. 15. Shook out.] As one shakes from the lap its contents. Compare Job 38 : 13 (revised version, and the writer's note).

17 To him who smote great kings;
For his mercy is forever;
18 And slew famous kings;
For his mercy is forever;
19 Sihon, king of the Amorites;
For his mercy is forever;
20 And Og, king of Bashan;
For his mercy is forever;
21 And gave their land for a heritage;
For his mercy is forever;
22 A heritage for Israel his servant;
For his mercy is forever.
23 Who in our low estate remembered us;
For his mercy is forever;
24 And rent us from our foes;
For his mercy is forever.
25 Who gives bread to all flesh;
For his mercy is forever.
26 Give thanks to the God of heaven;
For his mercy is forever.

PSALM CXXXVII.

1 By the streams of Babylon,
There we sat, and wept,
When we remembered Zion.
2 On willows in her midst,
We hanged our harps.

V. 1. Babylon.] Here, the province of Babylonia, through which the captives were dispersed.

V. 2. Willows.] The weeping willow is meant, which grew by the water-courses (Is. 44 : 4, 15 : 7; Job 40 : 22; Lev. 23 : 40).*

* The last reference suggests the occasion here referred to; namely, the great *feast of ingathering* (Ex. 23 : 16) commemorative of the harvest just gathered, and also of the deliverance from Egypt (Lev. 23 : 39–43); when "*willows of the brook*" (Lev. 23 : 40) were borne in procession, as part of the joyful pageant. This season of festivity was now turned to mourning; and their harps hung silent on the willows, once borne in triumph. Such a season of mourning seems alluded to in Ezek. 3 : 15, compared with Lev. 23 : 41.

3 For there demanded of us
Our captors, words of song,
And our oppressors, mirth:
Sing to us of the songs of Zion.
4 How shall we sing Jehovah's song,
On an alien soil!
5 If I forget thee, O Jerusalem,
Let my right hand forget!
6 Let my tongue cleave to my palate,
If I do not remember thee;
If I prefer not Jerusalem,
Above my chief joy.
7 Remember, O Jehovah, to the sons of Edom,
The day of Jerusalem;
Who said: Lay bare, lay bare,
To the very foundation therein.
8 Daughter of Babylon, the desolated!
Happy he who shall requite to thee,
Thy deed which thou hast done to us.
9 Happy he who shall seize,
And dash thy little ones against the rock.

PSALM CXXXVIII.

[Psalm] of David.

1 I WILL thank thee with my whole heart;
Before the gods will I sing praise to thee.
2 I will worship toward thy holy temple,
And will thank thy name for thy mercy and for thy truth;
For thou hast magnified thy saying above all thy name.
3 In the day when I called, then thou didst answer me,
Didst embolden me with strength in my soul.

V. 8. The desolated.] In prophetic anticipation.

V. 2. Thy saying.] See 2 Sam. ch. vii., to which reference is here made.

4 All kings of the earth will acknowledge thee, O Jehovah,
When they hear the sayings of thy mouth;
5 And will sing of the ways of Jehovah,
That great is the glory of Jehovah.
6 For exalted is Jehovah; and the lowly he regards;
And the proud he knows afar off.
7 Though I walk in the midst of trouble, thou wilt revive me;
Against the anger of my enemies thou wilt stretch forth thy hand,
And thy right hand will save me.
8 Jehovah will complete it in my behalf;
Jehovah, thy mercy is forever.
The works of thy hands do not forsake!

PSALM CXXXIX.

To the chief Musician. A Psalm of David.

1 JEHOVAH, thou hast searched me, and thou knowest.
2 Thou, thou dost know my sitting down and my rising up;
Thou perceivest my thought from afar.
3 Thou art around my path and my couch,
And art acquainted with all my ways.
4 For there is not a word in my tongue,
But lo, Jehovah, thou knowest it all.
5 Behind and before thou hast beset me,
And laid thy hand upon me.
6 Knowledge too wonderful for me!
It is high, I do not comprehend it.

V. 8. Will complete it. What he has purposed and begun, already referred to in v. 2.

V. 4. In my tongue.] In its power to utter, and as yet unuttered. Some translate, on my tongue. But to know a word that is already on the tongue implies no superhuman knowledge.

7 Whither shall I go from thy spirit?
And whither shall I flee from thy presence?
8 If I ascend into heaven, thou art there;
If I make the underworld my bed, lo thou art there.
9 If I should take the wings of the morning,
Should dwell in the uttermost part of the sea;
10 There also would thy hand lead me,
And thy right hand would hold me.
11 And if I say: Only let darkness cover me,
And the light about me be night;
12 Even darkness will not hide from thee,
And night will shine as the day;
Darkness is as light.
13 For thou, thou hast formed my reins,
Hast woven me in the womb of my mother.
14 I will praise thee, for I am fearfully, wonderfully made.
Wonderful are thy works;
And my soul knows it well.
15 My frame was not hidden from thee,
When I was made in secret,
Was curiously wrought [as] in the depths of the earth.
16 Thine eyes saw my unformed substance;
And in thy book were all of them written,
Day by day were they fashioned, when there were none of them.
17 And to me how precious are thy thoughts, O God!
How great is their sum!
18 If I would recount them, they are more in number than the sand;
I awake, and am still with thee.
19 O that thou wouldst slay the wicked, O God!
And ye men of blood, depart from me;
20 Who speak of thee with evil purpose,
Take [thy name] in vain,—thy foes.

V. 13. Reins.] The seat of perception and sensibility (Pss. 16 : 7; 73 : 21). They can conceal nothing from him who formed them. Compare Ps. 7 : 9.

21 Shall not I hate them, O Jehovah, that hate thee?
And shall I not loathe them that rise up against thee?
22 With perfect hatred do I hate them;
I count them my enemies.
23 Search me, O God, and know my heart;
Try me, and know my thoughts;
And see if there be any idol-way in me,
And lead me in the way everlasting.

PSALM CXL.

To the chief Musician. A Psalm of David.

1 RESCUE me, Jehovah, from the evil man;
From the violent man preserve me;
2 Who devise evil in the heart,
Continually they stir up wars.
3 They have sharpened their tongue like a serpent;
Poison of an adder is under their lips. (*Pause.*)
4 Keep me, O Jehovah, from the hands of the wicked;
From the man of violence preserve me;
Who have thought to subvert my steps.
5 The proud have hid a snare for me, and cords;
They have spread a net by the way-side;
Traps have they set for me. (*Pause.*)
6 I have said to Jehovah: Thou art my God;
Give ear, O Jehovah, to the voice of my supplications.
7 Jehovah, Lord, the strength of my salvation,
Thou hast covered my head in the day of battle.
8 Grant not, O Jehovah, the desires of the wicked man;
Do not further his device, that they may be lifted up. (*Pause.*)
9 As for the head of them that compass me about,
The mischief of their own lips shall cover them.

V. 23, 3d member. Idol-way.] Leading my heart from God, its supreme object of love.

10 Burning coals shall be cast down upon them ;
He will plunge them in fire ; into deep waters, that they rise not again.
11 An evil speaker shall not be established in the earth ;
The man of violence, evil will hunt him to ruin.
12 I know that Jehovah will maintain the cause of the sufferer,
The right of the poor.
13 Surely the righteous shall give thanks to thy name ;
The upright shall dwell in thy presence.

PSALM CXLI.

A Psalm of David.

1 Jehovah, I call upon thee ; make haste to me ;
Give ear to my voice, when I call to thee.
2 Let my prayer present itself as incense before thee ;
The lifting of my hands as the evening offering.
3 Set a guard, O Jehovah, at my mouth ;
Keep watch over the door of my lips.
4 Do not incline my heart to any evil thing,
To busy itself in wicked deeds,
With men that work iniquity ;
And let me not eat of their dainties.
5 Let the righteous smite me, it is kindness ;
And let him reprove me, it is oil for the head.
Let not my head refuse ; for still,
My prayer is in their calamities.
6 When their judges are hurled down among the rocks,
Then they hear my words, that they are pleasant.
7 As when one furrows and cleaves in the earth,
Our bones are scattered at the mouth of the underworld.
8 For my eyes are unto thee, Jehovah, Lord ;
In thee have I trusted ; do not pour out my soul.

V. 8. Pour out my soul.] Compare Is. 53 : 12, "poured out his soul."

9 Keep me from the grasp of the snare they have laid for me,
And the traps of the workers of iniquity.
10 Let the wicked fall into their own nets,
Until I shall have wholly passed by.

PSALM CXLII.

Didactic [Psalm] of David. When he was in the cave. A prayer.

1 WITH my voice to Jehovah I cry;
With my voice to Jehovah I make supplication;
2 I pour out before him my complaint,
My trouble I make known before him;
3 When my spirit faints within me,
And thou, thou knowest my path.
In the way that I go they have hidden a snare for me.
4 Look on the right hand and see,—and I have none that knows me;
Refuge has failed me;
There is no one that cares for my soul.
5 I cried unto thee, O Jehovah;
I said: Thou art my refuge,
My portion in the land of the living.
6 Be attentive to my cry, for I am brought very low.
Rescue me from my persecutors,
For they are stronger than I.
7 Bring out my soul from prison,
To thank thy name.
The righteous will gather round me;
For thou wilt deal kindly with me.

V. 10, 2d member. *Or*, Whilst I at the same time shall pass by.

Ps. cxlii. (title). In the cave.] Compare Ps. lvii; and see 1 Sam. 22 : 1 (with Dr. Hackett's addition to the art. Adullam, in *Smith's Bible Dictionary*) and 1 Sam. 24 : 3.

PSALM CXLIII.

A Psalm of David.

1 O JEHOVAH, hear my prayer;
Give ear to my supplications.
In thy faithfulness, answer me in thy righteousness.
2 And do not enter into judgment with thy servant;
For in thy sight no one living is righteous.
3 For the enemy has persecuted my soul,
Has smitten down my life to the earth,
Has made me dwell in darkness as those long dead.
4 And my spirit in me faints,
My heart is desolate within me.
5 I remember the days of old;
I meditate on all thou doest,
I think on the work of thy hands.
6 I spread out my hands unto thee;
My soul is as a land thirsting for thee. (*Pause.*)
7 Make haste to answer me, O Jehovah;
My spirit fails.
Do not hide thy face from me,
So that I become like them that go down to the pit.
8 Let me hear thy loving-kindness in the morning,
For in thee do I trust.
Make me know the way that I should go,
For to thee do I lift up my soul.
9 Rescue me from my enemies, O Jehovah;
With thee I hide myself.
10 Teach me to do thy will,
For thou art my God;
Let thy good Spirit guide me on even ground.
11 For thy name's sake, O Jehovah, thou wilt revive me;
In thy righteousness thou wilt bring my soul out of trouble.
12 And in thy loving-kindness thou wilt cut off my enemies,
And wilt destroy all that afflict my soul;
For I am thy servant.

V. 10, 3d member. Compare Ps. 26 : 12, "My foot stands in an even place."

PSALM CXLIV.

[A Psalm] of David.

1 BLESSED be Jehovah, my rock;
He who instructs my hands for the conflict,
My fingers for the battle;
2 My loving-kindness and my fortress,
My high tower, and my deliverer,
My shield, and in him I trust;
He that subdues my people under me.
3 Jehovah, what is man, that thou shouldst know him,
A son of man, that thou shouldst think of him?
4 Man is like a breath;
His days as a passing shadow.
5 Jehovah, bow thy heavens, and come down;
Touch the mountains, that they smoke.
6 Cast forth lightning, and scatter them;
Send out thine arrows, and discomfit them.
7 Send thy hands from on high,
Wrest me, and rescue me out of the great waters,
Out of the hand of aliens.
8 Whose mouth speaks deception,
And their right hand is a right hand of falsehood.
9 O God, a new song will I sing to thee;
With a ten-stringed lute will I sing praise to thee.
10 Who gives deliverance to kings;
Who wrests David, his servant, from the hurtful sword.
11 Wrest me, and rescue me from the hand of aliens;
Whose mouth speaks deception,
And their right hand is a right hand of falsehood.
12 So that our sons may be as plants,
Full grown in their youth;
Our daughters as corner pillars,
Sculptured after the structure of a palace;
13 Our garners full, supplying of every kind;
Our flocks multiplying by thousands,
By tens of thousands, in our fields;

14 Our oxen laden;
No breaking in, nor going forth,
And no outcry in our streets.
15 Happy the people to whom it is thus;
Happy the people whose God is Jehovah!

PSALM CXLV.

A Hymn of David.

1 I WILL extol thee my God, O king,
And will bless thy name forever and ever.
2 Every day will I bless thee,
And praise thy name forever and ever.
3 Great is Jehovah, and greatly to be praised,
And his greatness is unsearchable.
4 Generation to generation shall praise thy works,
And shall declare thy mighty acts.
5 The glorious honor of thy majesty,
And thy wondrous works will I sing.
6 And the might of thy terrible acts let them tell;
And thy great deeds will I rehearse.
7 Let them pour forth the memory of thy great goodness,
And sing aloud of thy righteousness.
8 Gracious and compassionate is Jehovah;
Slow to anger, and of great mercy.
9 Jehovah is good to all,
And his compassions are over all his works.
10 Let all thy works praise thee, O Jehovah,
And thy saints bless thee.
11 Let them tell the glory of thy kingdom,
And speak of thy power;

V. 14, 1st member. Laden.] With the abundant products of the fields.

V. 14, 2d member. "Breaking in," of invading armies, "going forth," into captivity, is most probably the meaning.

12 To make known to the sons of men his mighty acts,
And the glorious majesty of his kingdom.
13 Thy kingdom is a kingdom of all ages,
And thy dominion is throughout all generations.
14 Jehovah upholds all the falling,
And raises up all that are bowed down.
15 The eyes of all wait for thee,
And thou givest them their food in its season;
16 Opening thy hand,
And satisfying the desire of every living thing.
17 Righteous is Jehovah in all his ways,
And kind in all his works.
18 Near is Jehovah to all that call upon him,
To all that call upon him in truth.
19 He will fulfill the desire of them that fear him;
Their cry he will hear, and will save them.
20 Jehovah preserves all that love him;
And all the wicked he will destroy.
21 My mouth shall speak the praise of Jehovah;
And let all flesh bless his holy name,
Forever and ever.

PSALM CXLVI.

1 PRAISE ye JAH.
Praise Jehovah, O my soul.
2 I will praise Jehovah while I live;
I will sing praise to my God while I am in being.
3 Trust not in princes,
In a son of man, in whom there is no help.
4 His breath goes forth, he returns to his earth;
In that very day his plans perish.
5 Happy he, whose help is the God of Jacob,
Whose hope is in Jehovah his God;

6 Who made heaven and earth,
The sea, and all that is in them;
Who keeps truth forever;
7 Doing justice to the oppressed,
Giving food to the hungry.
Jehovah sets free the bound;
8 Jehovah opens the eyes of the blind;
Jehovah raises the bowed down.
Jehovah loves the righteous.
9 Jehovah preserves the strangers;
The orphan and widow he relieves;
And the way of the wicked he subverts.
10 Jehovah will reign forever,
Thy God, O Zion, to all generations.
Praise ye JAH.

PSALM CXLVII.

1 PRAISE ye JAH.
For it is good to sing praise to our God;
For it is pleasant, praise is becoming.
2 Jehovah builds Jerusalem,
The outcasts of Israel he will gather;
3 The physician for the broken in heart,
And he binds up their pains.
4 He counts the number of the stars;
He calls them all by their names.
5 Great is our Lord, and of great power;
His understanding is infinite.
6 Jehovah raises up the lowly;
He humbles the wicked even to the earth.
7 Answer Jehovah with thanksgiving,
Sing praise to our God with the harp;
8 Who covers the heavens with clouds,
Who prepares rain for the earth;

9 Who makes the mountains put forth grass,
Gives to the beast his food,
To the young ravens which cry.
10 He delights not in the strength of the horse,
Nor has he pleasure in the legs of men.
11 Jehovah has pleasure in them that fear him,
In them that hope in his mercy.
12 Praise Jehovah, O Jerusalem;
Praise thy God, O Zion.
13 For he has strengthened the bars of thy gates;
He has blest thy sons within thee.
14 It is he that makes thy borders peace;
He satisfies thee with the marrow of the wheat.
15 He that sends his commandment to the earth;
Swiftly does his word run.
16 He that gives snow like wool;
He scatters the hoar-frost like ashes.
17 He that casts forth his ice like morsels;
Who can stand before his cold?
18 He sends out his word and melts them;
He causes his wind to blow, the waters flow.
19 He makes known his word to Jacob,
His statutes and his judgments to Israel.
20 He has not done so to any nation;
And his judgments, they know them not.
Praise ye Jah.

PSALM CXLVIII.

1 Praise ye Jah.
Praise Jehovah from the heavens;
Praise him in the heights.

V. 10, 1st and 2d members. Horse and foot are meant, the cavalry and infantry of an army.

V. 14. Marrow of the wheat.] See the remark on Ps. 81 : 16.

2 Praise him, all his angels;
Praise him, all his hosts.
3 Praise him, sun and moon;
Praise him, all ye stars of light.
4 Praise him, ye heavens of heavens,
And ye waters that are above the heavens.
5 Let them praise the name of Jehovah;
For he commanded, and they were created;
6 And he made them stand forever and ever;
He set a bound, and they shall not pass over.
7 Praise Jehovah, from the earth;
Ye sea-monsters, and all deeps;
8 Fire and hail, snow and vapor,
Stormy wind fulfilling his word;
9 Ye mountains and all hills,
Fruit-trees, and all cedars;
10 Beasts, and all cattle,
Creeping things, and winged birds;
11 Kings of the earth, and all peoples,
Princes, and all judges of the earth;
12 Young men, and also maidens,
Old men, with children;
13 Let them praise the name of Jehovah;
For exalted is his name alone,
His majesty is above earth and heaven.
14 And he raised up a horn for his people,
A praise for all his saints,
For the sons of Israel, a people near to him.
Praise ye JAH.

PSALM CXLIX.

1 PRAISE ye JAH.
Sing to Jehovah a new song,
His praise in the congregation of saints.

V. 6, 2d member. *Or*, He made a decree, and it shall not pass.

2 Let Israel rejoice in his Maker,
The sons of Zion exult in their king.
3 Let them praise his name in the dance;
Let them sing praise to him with timbrel and harp.
4 For Jehovah has pleasure in his people;
He beautifies the lowly with salvation.
5 Let the saints triumph in glory,
Let them sing aloud upon their beds;
6 Praises of God in their throat,
And a two-edged sword in their hand;
7 To execute vengeance on the heathen,
Punishments on the peoples;
8 To bind their kings with chains,
And their nobles with fetters of iron;
9 To execute upon them the judgment written.
It is an honor for all his saints.
Praise ye JAH.

PSALM CL.

1 PRAISE ye JAH.
Praise God in his sanctuary;
Praise him in the expanse of his power.
2 Praise him for his mighty acts;
Praise him according to his abundant greatness.
3 Praise him with sound of trumpet;
Praise him with lute and harp.
4 Praise him with timbrel and dance;
Praise him with strings and pipe.
5 Praise him on the loud cymbals;
Praise him on cymbals of lofty sound.
6 Let all breath praise JAH.
Praise ye JAH.

THE END.

WORKS prepared by T. J. CONANT for the American Bible Union, and referred to in his Notes.

THE BOOK OF JOB; Part First, containing the Hebrew Text, the Common English Version, and a Revised Version, with a Critical Introduction, and Critical and Philological Notes. 1 vol. 4to.

THE BOOK OF JOB; Part Second, the Revised Version, with an Introduction and Explanatory Notes for English readers. 1 vol. 4to.

THE GOSPEL BY MATTHEW; containing the Greek Text, the Common English Version, and a Revised Version, with an Introduction and Critical and Philological Notes. 1 vol. 4to.

BAPTIZEIN; its Meaning and Use, Philologically and Historically Investigated. 1 vol. 8vo.

THE BOOK OF GENESIS; Revised Version, with an Introduction and Explanatory Notes. 1 vol. 8vo.

THE PSALMS; Revised Version, with an Introduction and occasional Notes. 1 vol. 8vo.

THE BOOK OF PROVERBS; Part First, containing the Hebrew Text, the Common English Version, and a Revised Version, with a Critical Introduction and Critical and Philological Notes. 1 vol. 4to. (In press, 1870.)

THE BOOK OF PROVERBS; Part Second, the Revised Version, with an Introduction and Explanatory Notes for English readers. 1 vol. 4to. (In press, 1870.)

For sale at the American Bible Union Rooms, 32 Great Jones Street, New York.

www.ingramcontent.com/pod-product-compliance
Lightning Source LLC
LaVergne TN
LVHW050524100826
845148LV00002B/435

* 9 7 8 1 4 2 5 5 2 0 3 6 6 *